Enjoy Being You

Ex-vangelical – a Deconstruction

By Andrea Gardiner

Andrea Gardiner is hereby identified as author of this work in accordance with Section 77 of the Copyright, Designs and Patents Act 1988

A CIP record for this book is available from the Britisn Library.

Dedicated in memory of my kind and generous Grandfather,

Sydney George Wilson

Who first told me to "Enjoy being you."

Contents

Introduction

Dear Reader,

Perhaps, like me, you were born into conservative, evangelical Christian faith, or found your home there early on. At first, it felt like welcome, belonging, security and certainty. It gave mission and purpose to my life. It provided the opportunity to serve, and show kindness, generosity and selflessness. It promised great joy, purity and happiness for all eternity. I was told it was unconditional love.

And then, as life went on, the cracks began to show. To begin with, I was able to ignore them, or paper over them. My life as a missionary, wife and mother, was too invested in this set of beliefs and reliant on this religious community to be able to let the questions and doubts I had surface. I kept them firmly nailed down under the floor. I was an expert at denial and repression of my true emotions. People-pleaser firmly in place, I soldiered on, submitting, serving and belonging.

Until I felt utterly and completely overwhelmed. The trapdoor in the floor burst open, and all my doubts and hurt erupted. I could no longer authentically stand before the congregation and speak the words they wanted to hear. I could no longer sing the lyrics of the worship songs without sobs shaking me. I could no longer live in this framework I had been given. It felt like a prison, a cage, a trap. I needed to find out who I was and what my true values and beliefs were, without being told that I had to believe what others defined the Bible as saying, or else.

I think I had to come to the end of myself to be able to go on this journey, because the fear was real. I feared God would send me to hell. I grieved being excluded by friends and family. I wondered if I could survive losing my identity and purpose as a missionary. What would be left, when all these things were taken away?

And yet, the years of damage, brokenness and wounds inflicted by harmful doctrines and teachings, that I had wholeheartedly embraced, could no longer be denied. I had to face them.

This book is a result of 3 years of deconstruction. I started feeling small, trapped, submissive, passive and fearful. I was never angry, always deferred to authority, especially male authority, always said "yes", and rarely gave my true opinion. I had never developed my own sense of self. I had no voice of my own. I let others define my roles. My life was lived out of an underlying fear of hell and punishment. I was trapped in a cycle of transactions, coercively controlled and had no experience of unconditional love.

I began to identify the doctrines, practices and teachings that had caused myself and many others such harm. I emptied them all out of my head and my heart, scattered them on the floor around me, examined them carefully and asked if these were compatible with Divine love.

I found new invitations of how to engage with mystery, identity, participating in God, the sacredness of all living things and Love.

The following pages are an offering of love to you. I will share my deconstruction of beliefs I have found to cause harm to ourselves and our neighbours. You are invited to consider them, examine whether they have also caused you, or your friends and community harm, and ask your own questions.

I will then offer different ways of encountering Divine Love, or your Higher Power. And I hope you will discover your own. My aim is not to bring you to the same conclusions I have come to (so far). It is to encourage you to ask questions. I am not trying to create a new set of doctrines or a statement of faith. I respect and embrace difference and diversity. My own beliefs continue to evolve. Rather, I am inviting you to reflect on how beliefs shape behaviour. Are they being weaponised, and causing harm? Or are they helping us love one another better?

If you have suffered harm from teachings such as those I discuss here, I hope these pages can assist you on your journey towards healing, wherever that takes you.

I would also just like to add a note about language used, before we begin. My own journey has involved oppression and abuse in a patriarchal, misogynistic culture, where God is male. As such, for me, the word "God", and using male pronouns for God unconsciously provokes negative emotions for me. I find it easier to relate to God by using words such as "Higher Power" or "Divine Love", and more inclusive pronouns including "she/her". I recognise that for some readers, such words might be problematic. I would ask you to use whichever terms you find most helpful.

Original Sin

"Then it was as if I suddenly saw the secret beauty of their hearts, the depths of their hearts where neither sin nor desire nor self-knowledge can reach, the core of their reality, the person that each one is in God's eyes. If only they could see themselves as they really are. If only we could see each other that way all the time, there would be no more war, no more hatred, no more cruelty, no more greed ... I suppose the big problem would be that we would fall down and worship each other."

Thomas Merton[1]

Deny yourself...

Self-compassion is sitting with me today. She whispers gently in my ear, as she gives me a hug. "You're tired and have been so busy recently. Take a day to rest. Do something fun!"

Immediately my old friend Deny Yourself rushes up in a panic. "You can't do that!" She screams. "You need to be busy serving others. There are people that need you today. It is very selfish to take time for yourself to rest. And you certainly can't waste your time having fun! God has done so much for you; you need to take up your cross and deny yourself for Him. And what will your family and friends think, if you just have a rest? They'll know you are a selfish, lazy, worthless person." I feel ashamed. Trapped. Exhausted.

And then I pause. "Oh, Deny Yourself, you've misunderstood! I was never meant to be a doormat, or to care so much for the needs of others that I neglect my own.

---

[1] Thomas Merton, *Conjectures of a Guilty Bystander* Image 1968

I don't find my worth or meaning in my service for others anymore. Addiction to busyness, my need to be needed, my pride at being the hero – all these things were false self, feeding my ego, but hiding my true valuable-just-because self.

Denying myself is a casting off of posturing, people-pleasing, consumerism and over-working. It is allowing myself to be freed from their bonds, to be healed of old wounds and freed to be my authentic self, with intrinsic value.

Self-compassion is teaching me I am just as human, just as valuable, as everyone else. She is showing me how to care for myself, forgive myself, and receive healing. She is teaching me to love and value myself." I take a deep, slow breath, right down into my abdomen. "And I feel whole. And I can give myself permission to rest. And to have fun. And I can then also let this transforming love and kindness flow gladly and generously to others."

****

Jesus said, "Whoever wants to be my disciple must deny themselves and take up their cross and follow me." Matthew 16:24 NIV

The command in this verse, at first glance, seems clear and inspiring. It appears to be a call to selflessness, to not looking to your own interests, but rather to those of other people. It encourages self-sacrifice, generosity and a willingness to suffer and even die for the benefit of others.

I think this interpretation can be a healthy challenge, if a person's starting point is that of entitlement and selfishness. However, I have also experienced and witnessed great harm coming from this teaching being given to children and adults whose starting point is a lack of self-worth. In these circumstances, being told to deny yourself is a recipe for burnout and oppression.

Perhaps, we simply need to be careful how we teach the ideal of selflessness. Maybe, we need communities where everyone is valued and encouraged to value themselves, alongside careful definitions of selfishness, in order to promote this idea, without causing harm.

However, I also think that maybe Jesus meant something quite different by this statement. Is it possible he was here alluding to that deeper inner journey of discipleship? This is the journey of denying your false self, which we enter into through suffering (our cross), and which frees us to live more and more wholeheartedly a life of love, as Jesus did (following him).

Let me explain what I mean. First, the harm this teaching can bring.

"Deny yourself" was a powerful part of the religious conditioning I received as a child, teen and grown woman in the Evangelical context and particular family and community I grew up in. I think gender had a large part to play in this, as the message was still, "Leadership in the church is male". Only men could have the status of priest/minister/elder in the churches I was a part of, and a woman was described as the "helpmate" of her spouse. Women and girls were encouraged to serve, but always ultimately under the authority of a man.

The perfect woman was one who served tirelessly and unconditionally, happy to be unnoticed and unappreciated. The more she did, and the more unobtrusively she did it, the greater her reward would be in heaven. She did not have needs, and certainly not wants. She deferred to others as default. To be holy, was to be utterly unselfish. Humility was considering yourself rubbish and others better than yourself.

This good Christian woman, who never needs anything for herself, is psychologically unhealthy. She does of course need some things for herself, she is simply repressing these needs. Not being allowed to express these needs, even to herself, leads to emotional problems, such as low mood and anxiety. If you need something, and cannot allow yourself to have that need met, you feel of little worth, and low. If the need is pressing, and you cannot admit that you need it, you become anxious. If you repress these emotions, your body becomes tense and has higher levels of stress hormones, which in turn lead to physical symptoms such as irritable bowel syndrome, migraines and palpitations.

You cannot pour from the proverbial empty cup. When a person serves tirelessly and unconditionally for too long, they burn out. When a person chronically pays no attention to their own needs, and only focuses on meeting the needs and wants of others, they will become exhausted and ill.

A person who believes themselves to be rubbish and that others are better than themselves, places themselves in a subordinate position, and is vulnerable to exploitation. Many such people will become people-pleasers, trying to gain approval and a sense of worth through their service for others, while chronically feeling guilty about doing anything to care for themselves. If an abusive person taps into this, it creates a never-ending cycle of taking advantage of the person, while reinforcing their low self-esteem.

When a community teaches this interpretation of "deny yourself" with a gender bias, it creates a culture where oppression can flourish. When men have automatic authority over women by virtue of their sex, and women are approved of when they serve selflessly, it is easy for women to end up manipulated, voiceless and powerless. This can be a contributory factor in domestic abuse, child abuse and sexual abuse occurring in Christian families.

I hope you can see that this seemingly virtuous teaching can, when wrongly applied, cause great harm.

And there is a deeper, even more damaging interpretation given to this idea of denying yourself also. This was the prayer we were encouraged to pray – "Oh Lord, here I am, wholly available. I just want to be what you want me to be, and do what you want me to do. I give up all my own desires and lay them at the foot of the cross. I slay them in Jesus' name. Just fill me and lead me in your path for me."

At the root of this teaching is the understanding that we are all worthless sinners, with nothing good to offer. This came from Augustine's doctrine of original sin: "Surely, I was sinful at birth, sinful from the time my mother conceived me."[2] It is the idea that only by completely subjugating ourselves, and ridding ourselves of our natural depraved, evil nature that we can be filled by the divine and be holy, good, worthy people.

I have seen this idea expressed by a picture of a man looking in a mirror and seeing a black sack full of rubbish. Pause with that for a moment and imagine the image. How does that make you feel?

What happens when a child grows up believing these teachings? As a child, I heard preachers say, "Yesterday my child disobeyed me. I never taught them to do this. It comes naturally to them. See what a depraved nature children are born with." Immediately, I felt shame. I was that child. "The only solution is to believe in Jesus. He died for you. He can make you clean. You must deny your natural desires. You must serve Him and be the person He wants you to be. He will probably ask you to do the very thing you least want to

---

2 Psalm 51 v 5 NIV

do, to test your love for Him. You must do it, and then there will be great rewards."

When this teaching is used to dominate and control, great harm can be done.

This child grows, believing themselves to be worthless rubbish. They believe they must do what their spiritual leaders tell them to. They suppress their own needs and wants. They feel dirty, evil and depraved. They must try and become holy, perfect and pure, but they know they are not as good as anyone else. Their true identity and personhood never develop. They neglect themselves. They become the people-pleaser, who is always busy doing things for their family, church and community. They can never stop, because then they are not good enough. They are full of shame.

Ironically, the help they offer to others is not coming from a place of loving kindness for others, even though it may appear to be on the surface – and indeed may well be what they think it is! It is driven by a need to be needed, not love. They are ultimately not seeking the good of the other person, but their own validation.

An example of this would be when I was running a charity and was also a mother of young children. People would tell me I was amazing for doing so much for other people. Yet, in reality my need to be needed and valued by others was such that I would prioritise the charity work, to the detriment of my own children's needs.

We notice this at work also when someone is helping us, but it feels like they are crossing boundaries or sucking us dry. The person presses unwanted gifts upon us, helps us when we are not asking for help, or imposes their solutions. And then they are hungry for appreciation in return.

How different it feels, how much healthier the dynamic, when the person serving or helping is secure in their own worth. They are able to respect our boundaries. They are able to prioritise their own needs and give from a place of genuine compassion and empathy, that imparts a sense a dignity and respect. They know how to give, and also how to receive. They show true humility; they have a realistic sense of their own strengths and weaknesses and value the strengths of others. They can be vulnerable. They give us a sense of equality. We never feel pitied by them.

Conversely, when someone believes they are garbage, they are very vulnerable to exploitation and abuse. Children who lack self-worth will look for something or someone to make them feel better about themselves – whether that is a substance, controlling their eating, becoming a workaholic or an unhealthy relationship. Women stay in abusive relationships in our churches, because they believe their husbands when they tell them that they are worthless. After all, isn t that what God says about them?

Do we really believe our sin cancelled out God's statement in Genesis 1, that humans are "very good"? Let's see what happens if we come to "deny yourself" from a different starting point.

When we start with the idea that we were created/born as good, beloved people, a different story unfolds. The goal is not to deny who we really are. The goal is to let our true, Beloved, soul shine.

As we go through life, we are wounded and develop defence mechanisms. These become a kind of false self. For example, someone who does not experience unconditional love from their parents may develop a people-pleasing false self. They become anxious to please and placate. They try hard to achieve and help others, in their thirst for approval and validation.

Or maybe someone who is falsely accused and judged by others develops a fear of what other people are thinking and saying about them, and withdraws and isolates themselves. They develop an anxious, socially phobic false self.

Or perhaps someone who is striving to find their worth in success at work and wealth develops an entitled, prideful false self.

I am sure you can think of others in yourself and your companions.

What if "deny yourself" means becoming aware of these false selves[3] in ourselves, and getting to know them? This self-awareness, together with a strong sense of our inherently loved and worthy personhood, allows us to have compassion on ourselves, and heal the wounds of our past. We might need the help of dear friends, pastoral care or a therapist to do this important inner work.

As we heal these wounds, we will find our false selves transform. We no longer need to defend ourselves. We can open ourselves with more vulnerability to love. We find the courage to show up in the world as our authentic selves. We can give our true gifts to ourselves and others. Our voice develops and contributes.

When the next cross we need to bear comes along in our lives, we are more able to respond with true compassion. If it is still important to you, we are more able to follow the example of Jesus and his unconditional love.

---

[3] To learn more about the concept of false self I recommend Immortal Diamond by Richard Rohr

Our true, wonderful self will be able to develop and shine more and more, blessing communities with its presence and giving its unique contribution to this world.

What if Christian communities were places where people discovered how precious and valuable, they are? What would happen if original blessing, rather than, or at least as well as original sin were preached from the pulpit? What would small groups be like if they were places where people could be vulnerable, able to share their shadow and their strengths, and together experience transformation? What would our communities feel like, were they filled with people who, secure in their own identity as Beloved, served each other with a sense of reverence and joy?

If you have been harmed by the doctrine "deny yourself", I hope this chapter has helped you look at it with a new lens. May you come to believe in your very bones, your intrinsic worth and the wonderful blessing that you are to our life here on planet earth. I hope you find the freedom to give yourself permission to have needs, express them and meet them. You are invited to join me on the journey of getting to know, love and accept ourselves, and in so doing, have a full cup, running over with love for other people.

Questions for reflection

Q1. How has "deny yourself" influenced you and your life?

Q2. What harm has this teaching done in your own life or community?

Q3. What do you think is a healthy way of applying this concept?

Q4. What do you think true humility means?

Q5. Can you think of any examples of defensive behaviours in your life? Describe how these have both helped and harmed your relationships.

Q6. What barriers are there to you showing up in the world as you really are?

Q7. What helps you find the courage to be vulnerable?

Q8. What fills your cup with the deep knowledge and acceptance that you are Beloved, just as you are? How can you nurture yourself?

Q9. What do you think causes burnout? How can we prevent it? How can we thrive?

Q 10. What do you think of the idea that denying myself is a casting off of posturing, people-pleasing, consumerism and over-working. It is allowing myself to be freed from their bonds, to be healed of old wounds and freed to be my authentic self, with intrinsic value?

Q11. What one thing can you do differently from now on, as a result of this chapter?

Sacrifice

When I was a teenager, I was an avid reader of missionary biographies. One of the biographies I read several times was that of Keith Green: No Compromise. He was an American singer-songwriter, and I listened to his music all the time. Here is part of one of his songs.

To obey is better than sacrifice
I don't need your money
I want your life
And I hear you say that I'm coming back soon
But you act like I'll never return

To obey is better than sacrifice
I want more than Sunday and Wednesday nights
Cause if you can't come to Me every day
Then don't bother coming at all …

And I'm coming quickly
To give back to you
According to what you have done[4]

His message was that people needed to give everything for Jesus, and to be willing to travel to the ends of the earth to spread the gospel, without counting the cost. He was lauded for his life of faith, and wanted as many people as possible to follow his example of being "sold out for Jesus."

A big part of his message and motivation was that life was short, and any discomfort now was insignificant, compared to the glory to come. He preached that the end of the world was near. Life in the here and now was unimportant. It was

---

[4] To Obey Is Better Than Sacrifice by Keith Green from the album No Compromise released 1978

simply urgent to evangelise as many as possible, as quickly as possible.

It was a heady message for a teenager, eager to please their Christian parents, and one I took to heart.

Keith Green died very young, in a tragic small airplane crash, along with 2 of his children. The plane was overloaded. Did he think God would prevent the tragedy waiting to happen? How would he and his children have further blessed the world had they lived longer? Would his message have mellowed with the years?

The idea that sacrificing your life for God was what God required of us was preached by many in their sermons. It built on the idea of denying yourself that we looked at in the first chapter. The premise that we are unworthy again undergirded this teaching. Added to the mix was this idea that life on planet earth had no value in itself other than as a chance to make a decision for Jesus, that would grant entry into eternal bliss. It created a real sacred/secular divide, where spiritual activity was considered to be of great value, while secular work and especially play were disregarded or even despised.

Some went so far as to teach that a person's happiness was of no consequence. It was framed as "We are NOT called to do what makes us happy. We're called to do what glorifies God."[5] Glorifying God was said to mean obeying God, obeying parents and other authority figures, doing our duty, making sure we did not damage the witness of the church, sacrificing ourselves, all the while paying no attention to our emotions or personal happiness.

---

[5] Meme seen on Facebook

The idea of sacrifice is central to Christianity, and is glorified. It permeates Christian ideology and is the driving force, or excuse, for many a decision. Sometimes, it is a beautiful thing, when done with love, freely, and within the context of healthy balance. As we saw with Deny Yourself, when a person starts with a healthy sense of self, and the ability to set appropriate boundaries, choosing to sacrifice your time, energy, and resources for the good of your neighbour is a blessing to all.

However, I think we need to recognise that in other circumstances, teaching people to sacrifice does untold harm. More often that we might like to suppose, it is used to control, pressure or coerce.

Many church leaders teach, even urge, their congregations to sacrifice their time, money, gifts and talents for God and the programmes the church is running. "Your reward is in heaven", they proclaim. "It does not matter if you are happy in this life. In heaven you will be full of joy for all eternity. So, sacrifice yourself now, and you will gain these great rewards." And sacrificing yourself can feel very virtuous. The person can feel useful, of value and full of purpose. They feel they are making a contribution to a higher cause.

And there is always plenty to be done, of course. The poor are always with us. The children need Sunday School teachers. The youth need leaders. The tea and cake after church is always appreciated. The food bank needs run. The housebound need visitors. The list is endless. And that is without thinking of the foreign missions, climate change action and prayer meetings. Many people are able to freely, willingly and lovingly give their time and money to these causes.

And then, the balance starts to tip. Pressure is applied. Guilt kicks in. Everyone else seems to contribute so much more, we feel like a second-class Christian. People start to sacrifice more than they have to give, out of a sense of shame, or because they believe they should deny themselves, and believe they can have no boundaries. Maybe they believe the end of the world is imminent, and that their reward is in heaven. Perhaps they think it is what God requires of them. Maybe they worry what other people think of them. Often people give to excess because they feel the need to prove their worth, or gain love and approval. Sacrifice becomes driven by fear, duty and guilt.

And so, there is the destitute woman who relies on her neighbours to feed her children, giving the pittance she does possess to the Pentecostal pastor who tells her that this will give her favour with God. There is the mother who spends so much time running the creche, mothers and toddlers and coffee morning at church, as well as working part time, that she has no time with her own children. There is the single female missionary who repeatedly goes to a dangerous part of the city alone, because she is "called by God, and God will protect her." Until she is sexually assaulted. There is the 8-year-old child sobbing themselves to sleep each night in a boarding school, because this is a sacrifice their parents have decided to make in order to share the gospel in a foreign land, and after all, the teachers at the missionary school have been called to care for their children. There is the wife sacrificing her own well-being by not speaking up about her husband's abusive behaviour at home, because he is such a pillar of the church and does so much good there. The Christian worker/pastor/missionary burns out because they can never actually do enough to earn love, approval and self-worth. Rest and play feel shameful to them.

I think we need to be very careful when we notice we are doing something out of a noble sense of sacrifice. If we scratch below the surface, the motivation is often actually our need to be needed, appreciated or accepted. It is not love. We need to question whether it is actually causing ourselves, or others, harm.

I now believe that we can only truly love others as much as we love ourselves. Maybe, like me, you were taught the JOY acronym; Jesus, Others, Yourself. The idea was that we should put Jesus first, then look to the needs of others, and only then think of our own needs.

Jesus actually taught us to love others *as we love ourselves.* Think about people you know who do take care of themselves, just as much as they do other people. Those I know who do this are generally content, calm, joyful people, who are open and generous and full of compassion. They say "no" to some things asked of them, with great grace, and signpost the person to other avenues of help. When they say "no" or "not now" to me, I never feel dismissed or unloved. I am assured of their concern and respect their ability to set boundaries. Our friendships last.

In contrast, when I was the "yes" missionary doctor, and paid no attention to my own needs, I ended up hiding to avoid being asked yet another favour. I was exhausted and running in top gear 24/7. I gave instant responses, and rarely saw the deeper needs of those around me, or the bigger, systemic issues. I was defensive, on a short fuse and cut people off when their demands overwhelmed me.

I cannot express how different it feels to learn to love yourself, and have compassion on yourself. How freeing it is to acknowledge that you cannot do it all, and to burst out of the chains of should, must and have to. The more profoundly I know that I am doing the best I can, and that that is enough, the more I can extend that same belief to other people. My body is more relaxed, pain free and healthy. My spirit is filled with joy. My mind is open and curious.

I am able to consider which tasks are mine to do, and give my true gifts to the world, without guilt about those I turn down.

When we are taught self-sacrifice, without boundaries, it creates a part of us called, "Don't feel". Whenever anything feels remotely uncomfortable, upsetting, painful, or, God-forbid, anger-inducing, Don't Feel jumps right in and stuffs the emotion down and out of sight. He slaps a smile on our faces and tells us sternly to grin and bear it.

Don't Feel taught me that my happiness was not important. He taught me that my feelings were not important. Therefore, I felt that I was not important.

I believed it was important to glorify God. Glorifying God, of course, was defined by others. It was used to require blind obedience. It was used to coercively control.

When a person suppresses their emotions, they do not disappear. They come out in other ways. They twist a person's gut into irritable bowel syndrome. They blind a person with headaches. They erupt through their skin in an angry red rash. They attack the person in the form of autoimmune diseases. The pressure of them builds inexorably as high blood pressure. They suffocate the person with panic attacks. They crush their chest, they grip their shoulders, they take away their breath.[6] The person may be passive-aggressive, have flashes of terrifying, uncontrolled rage, or dissociate.

---

[6] To read more about trauma stored in the body I recommend The Body Keeps the Score by Bessel van der Kolk

When a person believes that they are not important, they continue living in harmful circumstances long after a healthy person would have left. They stay in the loveless marriage, the abusive relationship, the cult or the job where their boss is mistreating them.

"Glorifying God", can also be twisted to mean that doing church work is superior to doing secular work. It can give such church leaders a certain status, which the less scrupulous may use to obtain respect, privileges or to abuse their power.

"Glorifying God" can also be used to silence people when there are breaches of trust, abuse or wrong-doing in the church. It is then said to mean not letting other people know about human failings of Christians, otherwise it will damage the witness of the church and detract from God's glory. So, the dynamic is set up, where the church leader is revered as the person that brings glory to God through their divine work, and when they do something harmful to others, congregants will not speak up, because they fear it will damage the reputation of the church. They, and their happiness is not important, so why would they risk angering God? They are prepared to sacrifice themselves "for the greater good".

And this creates a toxic version of God. This cold, demanding God who needs to be glorified so much, that he/she does not care about human happiness.

Starting with original blessing enables us to value ourselves, our emotions and our happiness. Original blessing affirms Genesis 1v 31, which states that God saw that we and all creation were very good. It is in line with the Divine command to look after the world, here and now, and each other. I now firmly reject this notion that the only thing that matters in life is converting as many people as possible for a future after we die. I believe that life here and now; our flesh, born in a rush of blood and sweat, the earth squelching between our toes, the life-giving air we inhale with each breath and the thirst-quenching water that revives us and sustains us are all permeated with value and importance.

I believe that all of creation is sacred.[7] If you like, it is all God-breathed. Divine love and goodness infuse the blazing sunset, the colourful pansy and the faithful hound. I find that the more I pay attention to and honour the planet, by planting a bulb, reducing my consumption, or going for a walk along the cliffs, the more in tune I am with the rhythms of life. I no longer have to be doing something "spiritual" to feel it is of value. I can take time to appreciate nature's wonderful and gracious gifts in the here and now. I can value people as they are, here and now. I can hold space for suffering to be expressed, questions to be pondered over, and mystery to be accepted.

And the Higher Power I encounter is gentle and gracious. The Divine Love I experience in the ordinary every-day, rejoices in happiness and appreciates, but does not demand, generosity.

More than anything else, it is the breath-taking beauty of nature that I encounter as glorious, wondrous and awe-inspiring. The deep appreciation I feel for the blazing sunset and impressive view are what some call, "giving glory to God." It makes me feel grounded, joy-filled and complete. It sparks a desire to care for the well-being of nature and all who reside on this planet.

---

[7] To read more about this I recommend The Universal Christ by Richard Rohr

I firmly believe that God's glory is not protected through sacrifice, silence and cover-up. It delights in the truth, and shines a light on evil so that it can be transformed. It requires activism and courage.

I do not think God needs our sacrifices. That makes no sense at all, when the very definition of the Divine is wholeness. Before we start giving to a Higher Power, or others, we need to be secure in knowing that we are loved and accepted, just as we are, just because we exist, warts and all. And then we are ready to accept the invitation of participating in Divine extravagance.

I would like to finish this chapter with a special plea for us not to sacrifice our children. We need to stop and examine ourselves when we are thinking of doing something that involves sacrifice for our children. Or if we are teaching our children to sacrifice themselves, before they have a healthy sense of self and of their worth in the first place.

It is the work of childhood for a child to develop their own personhood and identity. They need a secure attachment from infancy in order to feel safe. When they grow understanding that they are accepted by their family just as they are, they have room to explore and discover their own gifts, personality and sense of self. As they come to adolescence, and push boundaries and experiment, they need a strong sense of belonging no matter what.

I think a healthy relationship with a Higher Power displays this same sense of secure attachment, and deep knowing that we are accepted and belong, just as we are and no matter what. It is called unconditional love.

When a child feels that their parents are sacrificing the child's needs to pursue their own goals, even if these seem noble or divine to the parent, the child is likely to feel not enough. They may develop protective parts of themselves to try to gain approval, or rebel in protest. If they are taught that they should sacrifice themselves for God, their development often becomes distorted.

This kind of spirituality easily becomes coercive. The child feels they only belong to their family and church community, if… If they accept Jesus, if they are baptised, if they are straight, if they never get drunk, if they remain a virgin until marriage, if they ignore themselves and are busy doing things for other people and the church all the time.

They may come to adulthood not knowing who they really are with little sense of their own values and true self. This can be very damaging to their psyche and lead to all sorts of emotional, behavioural, psychological and physical problems.

The potential for harm is huge and can affect them for many years.

As parents, we need to be able to prioritise the needs of our children. We need to make sure they know they are loved unconditionally. We need to teach them to feel their emotions, and value their happiness. We need to pay attention to their lives in the here and now, not just worry about whether they are going to heaven. They need to grow up feeling part of the wider human community. It is damaging to send them to school thinking that their job is to evangelise their school mates. We need to value their ordinary, everyday experiences and achievements, not just when they participate in the Sunday service.

We need to teach them to set boundaries and value themselves, so that they can protect themselves against exploitation, pressure and abuse. We need to teach them to speak up about anything that is upsetting them, and listen to them, not defend the institution or reputations of others.

When they understand that no one else has the right to demand self-sacrifice from them, they will be able to show up as kind, compassionate people without fear. They will have learnt what love really is. And having experienced this love for themselves, be able to share it with a sense of generosity, and sometimes sacrifice.

We need to value ourselves, model managing our emotions in a healthy manner, and value our time here on planet earth. We need to appreciate and enjoy the ordinary, as extraordinary gifts. We need to give time, space and love to our children. Becoming generous people, who sometimes sacrifice for others is great. But it does make us any more holy or important.

What if self-sacrifice is over-rated?

Maybe sticking to doing what is loving, healthy, and promotes the well-being of all, ourselves and our children included is a better place to start.

Questions for reflection.

Q1. What have you sacrificed in life?

Q2. Why do you think you did this? Was it from a sense of duty, coercion, love, compassion, something else?

Q3. Have you experienced burn-out? What did you learn through that experience?

Q4. Have you experienced being pressured to ignore your own happiness, remain silent, or stay in a destructive relationship? What happened? What resulted?

Q5. How have you encountered divine love? What is your God like? What does your God demand of you?

Q6. What do you want to teach your children about sacrifice?

Q7. Do you think sacred work has more value than secular work? Tell me about that…

Q8. What ordinary things do you enjoy and value in life? How can you nurture that?

Q9. Can you think of an example you have witnessed/experienced of a healthy, compassionate relationship or act of service? What was it like? What can you learn from that?

Q10. Do you think you are as valuable as your neighbour? Do you love yourself? Why or why not?

Anxiety and Fear

Christianity claims to be a religion that offers peace. We call Jesus the Prince of Peace. We proclaim Jesus created peace between our sinful selves and God. We describe our churches as refuges and loving communities. So why are so many Christians anxious? Why are so many Christian children growing up expressing their distress in self-harm, OCD, eating disorders, school-refusal and substance use? What are we all so afraid of?

At the start of the pandemic, we were reading a devotional as a family that asked the question, "Are you at peace?" Even as I opened my mouth to glibly reply, "yes", the realisation hit me right in the chest. I had no peace. I actually felt deeply conflicted, divided, compromised, exhausted, overwhelmed and anxious, despite being deeply committed to Jesus.

It was such a relief to finally admit it! And then get some help. And start reading, listening, pondering and questioning. These are some of the layers I discovered on my journey to inner peace.

First, I realised I had a fear-based faith. It was not grounded in unconditional love and acceptance.

Second, I understood I had suppressed my own values to be accepted by my religious community, and felt deeply conflicted and inauthentic. I said "yes" when I wanted to say "no". I remained silent when I needed to speak up. I had never developed my own voice, just parroted what others wanted to hear.

Third, I had learnt to people-please out of fear of what people were thinking of me and how they would react. I was afraid of rejection. This had been made even more complicated by being a missionary financially dependent on the good opinion of other Christians. I feared expressing my true opinions in case they stopped supporting me in my missionary work.

Fourth, I did not love myself. Deep down I felt that I was worthless.

Let's explore how these harmful, anxiety-producing beliefs can develop within a "Bible-believing" Christian community and upbringing, the harm they can do and alternative ways of seeing things.

Fear-based faith

Imagine you are a child and you are repeatedly told, "If you are not a Christian you are going to go to hell when you die." And, "the end of the world is coming soon, we are living in the end times. You need to be ready to be raptured at any moment. If you are not trusting in Jesus, you will be left behind and face terrible suffering." Perhaps you do not need to imagine this. Maybe, like me, you were brought up believing this. Did you also listen to sermons on Revelation, Daniel and the end times on your car journeys as a child? Or read the "Left Behind" series?

At the very least, this is fear-inducing. It should be no surprise if such children are anxious. Listen to the 5-year-old who goes to school believing their task is to evangelise their friends, because they are not Christians, so they are going to hell.

"I feel very anxious. All the other children think I am different and weird. No one wants to play with me. But I can't join in and be like them, because they will lead me into sin."

By the time they are 10, they can verbalise the existential trap they experience and the despondency it causes.

"I wish I had never been born. It is all a cruel joke. I never asked to exist. But here I am, and I now have to exist for all eternity. If I get the answer to the Jesus-riddle wrong, I am going to end up burning in hell forever. What kind of God made life this way? And there is no escape, even killing myself won't free me. I wish I had never been born."

This kind of belief in hell and punishment also invites superstition. Church leaders often speak out against superstition, laughing at people who fear Friday the 13th, or black cats crossing the road. But almost in the same breath they warn believers not to use the number 666, or to say the word "Santa" because it is an anagram of "Satan", or to put off baptising their baby in case they die an infidel. I've heard Christians say their children may not read books about fairies, because they come from paganism, nor Harry Potter nor other books about witches and wizards. This kind of teaching and behaviours are also fear-inducing, and feed anxiety. What kind of God would reject a baby because he or she had not been baptised? What kind of God is powerless before the number 666, or challenged by a fantasy story for children?

Similarly, speculation about the end of the world, and which war currently happening in the world is actually the work of the antichrist is unproductive and anxiety-provoking. It certainly does nothing to show solidarity with or help the victims of such wars.

In the same way, teaching on the occult and the demonic can be terrifying to a child. I remember being too afraid to even look at the page of a magazine with horoscopes on it, in case an angry lightning bolt struck me, and believed if I did yoga a demon would possess me as it allegedly involved "emptying my mind". A recent episode of Call the Midwife[8] did an excellent portrayal of how frightening prayer for exorcism can be for a child.

If a parent uses the threat of hell to control their child, for the benefit of the adult, then it is abuse. It is deeply damaging when a child is forced to comply because they are afraid, not only of their parents, but of God, who is all-seeing and omnipresent. The child will never develop their authentic personhood. Instead, they will develop mal-adaptive personality traits that are trauma responses.

If this happened to you, I am truly sorry. It was not your fault. It is possible to heal and find yourself, even now. Pause and grieve. Notice the emotions coming up for you, and express them. Then, keep reading. You do not need to live in fear any more.

If a parent truly believes in hell, and also loves their child, they will teach it from a place of love, trying to save their child from eternal damnation. Here, there is no intention to abuse their child. However, the teaching itself remains damaging. The child is very likely to grow up anxious. The parents, too, are likely to be anxious! It is very hard for such a parent to avoid putting pressure on their child to adopt their beliefs, as they truly believe the eternal stakes are so high. It is very difficult for the child to step back and question whether they also believe this, when they are caught up in a cycle of fervent belief and fear. It also creates a fear-inducing God. The child and parent "fear God", meaning they fear wrath and punishment. They are likely to be anxious to please and develop perfectionist tendencies. The damage is passed on from one generation to the next, until someone breaks the cycle.

---

[8] Call the Midwife Series 14 Episode 1

Pete Rollins says in the Divine Magician, "An insidious unbelief allows communities to get the psychological pleasure from the beliefs they hold without having to actually confront the horror of fully affirming them in a material way."[9] So, often people say, "I believe non-Christians are going to hell." But they are not desperately going around trying to convert everyone they meet. If they are really honest, they do not believe that can actually be true. They can enjoy the security that belief gives them, maybe even the sense of being "right" and "safe", without ever confronting the horror of believing their neighbour is going to burn in eternal torment.

So, these parents profess to believe in hell, but also give their children the space to question their faith. Perhaps it is not mentioned very often. The parents focus on loving their children, showing them kindness, encouraging them to thrive. Hell is never used as a threat in day-to-day life. Faith is more something that is lived out, than doctrines taught in words. The children know their parents will love them and be proud of them no matter what.

These people are not abusive and are much less likely to be anxious. Their children feel free to make their own choices about their beliefs. Sometimes, the belief of the parent will actually crumble when the unbelief is exposed. In this case, for example, it might be when their dearly loved, precious, non-Christian child dies in a motor-bike accident. There is no death-bed repentance. What do they believe then?

Spiritual abuse and harmful spirituality feel like absolutes, objectification, repression of emotions, oppression, violation of boundaries, prohibition of free thought and questions, no room for disagreement, entrapment, lack of self-worth,

---

[9] Pete Rollins *Divine Magician* Kindle edition 2015 p154

never good enough, obligation, exclusion, fear, pressure, control and coercion.

Healthy spirituality feels like an invitation, choices, spaciousness, freedom, liberation, expansion, curiosity, peace, awe, abundance, diversity, inclusivity, loving kindness and authenticity.

The belief that salvation is exclusive, only available to those who pray a sinner's prayer to Jesus, or to those who are baptised and confirmed, is constricting and limiting. The belief that everyone else is going to hell, a place of eternal torment, is fear-inducing. These beliefs are easily used to control people. They feel small and entrapping and restricting. They make this life something to endure, for the promise of eternal bliss in the future.

I stopped believing in hell because of the kind of God that belief creates. If I, as an ordinary human being, could not ever send anyone to eternal torment, no matter how evil they had been, how can I believe in a God who would do that? If God is like that, I would rather have nothing to do with him/her.

Richard Rohr also cites the infinite nature of life as one of his reasons for not believing in hell. Death is not infinite, so how can there be eternal death? He goes on to say, "Religion is lived by people who are afraid of hell. Spirituality is lived by people who have been through hell."[10]

I used to live in this religious way, taking the Bible literally, believing that salvation was a transaction. I lived in fear of eternal punishment, and living that way I would now describe as a living hell. It meant living inauthentically, (which is an existential torture), and that others could control

---

[10] Richard Rohr, *Breathing Underwater* Franciscan Media 2021

me and harm me. It was sold as grace, and then we had to spend a life time earning it religiously.

I am still a spiritual person, which for me now means the joy and wonder of experiencing the infinite possibilities of life here and now.

One day, I was driving my commute, when I noticed that the clock in the car had stopped. I let myself imagine that time was standing still. I instantly felt relaxed. I had all the time in the world to journey! Instead of worrying about getting to a destination on time, I could take my time. I could savour every moment and each experience along the way.

I don't know what happens after death. Actually, none of us do. But the moments, hours and days that I am fully present, enjoying life as it happens, open, curious, fearless and full of love, I feel I am living heaven on earth. These moments feel eternal.

Life itself feels so infinite. The universe seems to be without end. The details in flowers, snowflake designs, and patterns on giraffes all appear to be endless. The northern lights, distant stars and gleaming rainbows inspire awe. We marvel at the organisation of ants, the beauty of a coral reef and the sweetness of a raspberry. How can we conceive of there being an end to this boundless wonder?

And what about our loved ones: those we love extravagantly, without limit and without end? Surely love is eternal?

And the Higher Power of infinite love, beauty and welcome enables me to relax and be at peace. I would now describe "fearing God" as the awe this Divine experience inspires. I wonder at the unconditional love that accepts everyone and includes all diversity.

Belonging

When we have to conform to belong, we are fitting in, not living authentically aligned to our own values. We suppress our arguments and objections, stay silent and do not protest, for fear of expulsion and excommunication. We have no inner peace. We are contorting ourselves, and people-pleasing; mechanisms we develop to cope with our fear of rejection.

Let me give you an example. I was brought up in a Christian community that taught that God hates homosexuality. It was theorised that God could change people's sexual orientation if they prayed hard enough. Some practiced this in the form of conversion therapy, "abusive and harmful practices that seek to change or suppress a person's sexual orientation or gender identity."[11] Being Christian was incompatible with gay-marriage.

And then, as a young adult I actually met people who were gay, and they became friends. I listened to their lived experience that their orientation was not something that could change. They suffered terribly when others imposed their conversion views upon them, or rejected them. They found great love and happiness in same-sex relationships. I found it impossible to hold on to the view that for them to be accepted by the God who had made them, they needed to commit to a life of celibacy and loneliness, or become heterosexual.

However, this was such a key teaching of my faith community of origin, that they considered me back-slidden,

---

[11] **https://www.gov.scot/policies/lgbti/ending-conversion-practices** accessed 13.03.2025

or no longer a Christian for believing in gay rights. I was no longer part of their group.

Expressing our views and values can have huge consequences. It may mean we are no longer permitted to teach Sunday school, lead services or be respected in our local church. It may even mean having to leave a church or being rejected by our family. People who are working as pastors or missionaries may lose their employment.

The consequences can seem so immense that we understandably stay quiet and try to keep the peace. However, we will feel conflicted within. We will have no peace. We will feel anxious.

Healthy spirituality permits curiosity. It allows questions and new ways of seeing things. It is comfortable with the evolution of faith and prioritises the expression of love. It moves away from the history of slavery, sexism and homophobia towards wider love and equality. It is conscious we all have blinkers, biases and lenses through which we see the world. It embraces the journey that is life and the path of transformation.

How different it feels to be part of a faith community that, instead of building a fence around those who are "in", drinks deeply from the well of love and invites others to join them, and is open to learning from all who come.[12]

For those of us who grew up in faith communities that demanded conformity, we have a lot of unlearning to do. Conformity and Deny Yourself teach us to be "yes" people. We feel obliged to agree and take on whatever is asked of us. We believe that the command to "Love God with all your heart" means do everything your church leaders tell you to

---

[12] John Ortberg *Eternity is now in session* John Murray Press 2019

and devote as much time as possible to church activities. Our path to healing and inner peace requires us to learn how to set boundaries.

Prentis Hemphill says, "Boundaries are the distance at which I can love you and me simultaneously."

Many of us need to learn that "no" is a very necessary word, and is also a complete sentence.

Living and loving wholeheartedly means being able to truly express our views, agree to differ, ask our questions, attend to our own needs without guilt, and live in line with our own values (which may change over time!).

We need to be able to set boundaries with our faith community, when doctrines are being used to coerce us into going along with views and values we do not hold. We may need to leave Christian employment. Love does not coerce. Love invites and is spacious.

Boundaries are needed when we feel we are expected to give more time and resources than we have at that moment. Unconditional love is not earned. Getting burnt out is not the ultimate badge of devotion. Love allows rhythm and rest and fun.

If you are recovering from this kind of dogmatic in/out type of religion, you may need very firm boundaries at first. You may need to walk away completely, and not even talk to God for a while. Maybe a long while, as you sift through the rubble and allow your true self and values to emerge and become established as the calm, confident centre of you.

God can cope with you setting boundaries with him/her as well! Don't worry! There may need to be a big distance between you both while you learn to love yourself, after a lifetime of fear.

Perfect love casts out fear. Unconditional love is patient and kind, it rejoices with the truth, it always protects, always trusts, always hopes and always perseveres.[13] That kind of God will wait as long as is needed for you to feel safe and be able to trust and move closer. And when you are ready to approach, you may well be surprised to find you are sitting on the lawn together in the sunshine, picking daisies and chatting. Not rushing about trying to impress God, as you were before.

You may just find you no longer feel that exhausting fear and anxiety.

Self-Worth

Henri Nowen commented, "For a very long time I considered low self-esteem to be some kind of virtue. I had been warned so often against pride and conceit that I came to consider it a good thing to deprecate myself. But now I realise that the real sin is to deny God's first love for me, to ignore my original goodness."[14]

Living in a consumer society, we are groomed to think of ourselves as lacking something, so that we can be seduced into buying more and more in the belief that this will make us feel complete. Social media can create in us a fear of missing out.

A society that devalues the elderly, infirm and disabled wants us to believe that our worth is tied to our productivity. We need to work more hours and climb the career ladder to try and fill the chasm within.

---

[13] 1 Corinthians 13 v 7 NIV

[14] Henri Nouwen *The Return of the Prodigal Son* DLT 1994 p107

Television shows and media that laud and obsess over celebrities want us to believe that fame is the answer to low self-esteem. They encourage us to seek notoriety and recognition.

They all seek to manipulate and seduce us into doing, buying and being something we are not, because they convince us that what we are is inadequate.

Religion that tells us we are depraved sinners, with nothing good to offer God, does the same thing. It makes us small, so that we can be seduced and manipulated. It grooms us into working too hard, being who we are not, and putting our energy into polishing our image and reputation.

It has us running around trying to discover ways to find, know, love, deserve and impress God, when all along Jesus said that God is the shepherd who is out in the dark night searching for the lost sheep.

What if the truth is that we do not want God to know us as we are? What if we are afraid God will find us and discover we are dirty and small? What if we cannot let God love us, because we feel the need to earn that love? What if we still think of God as the judge, just waiting to zap us? What if we are afraid that we are worthless?

I would like to invite you to immerse yourself in the story of the Prodigal Son. Imagine you are the younger son, returning from that far off land. Think about the failures, rejections and sadness you have experienced in life. Name them in your mind. Feel them in your body.

What are you rehearsing in your head to negotiate, to be allowed back home? What can you offer? What would you like to ask for? What kind of reception are you expecting from the parent you abandoned?

Lift your head and see the figure flying down the dusty road to meet you, joy lighting up their face. Stop your trudging. Feel the love pouring towards you. What resistance do you feel? What is stopping you from receiving this unconditional love?

Can you lay this burden down, and receive love? Can you allow yourself to be known? Will you run away – or allow yourself to be found?

Questions for reflection.

Q1. What kind of higher power/God do you believe in?

Q2. What does fearing God mean to you?

Q3. What do you believe about eternity, heaven and hell?

Q4. Have you experienced fear as a result of your religious beliefs? How?

Q5. Are you free to have questions and hold your own values in your faith community? How does that feel?

Q6. Have you ever experienced rejection or exclusion by your faith community? What happened and how did it feel?

Q7. What does true belonging look like?

Q8. What effect does your belief system have on your self-worth?

Holiness & Perfectionism

I made a mistake. Inner critic is going to town on me. "How could you slip up like that? You need to take a long, hard look at yourself! You call yourself a good Christian woman, and then go and do that! You're a hypocrite. Everyone will think you are so bad for doing that. You should be ashamed of yourself. You are useless."

I am drowning in a pool of shame, regret, despondence and depression. I am frozen. I am never going to be good enough. I am supposed to be perfect.

Loving Kindness comes alongside me and gently challenges me. "Would you speak to your friend or your children like that?" she probes. The fog begins to lift as I raise my gaze and take in my surroundings. I feel the ground I am sitting on, and wiggle my toes. I take a deep, slow breath and remember I am no longer a child, who is told to aim for perfection every day, and shamed for failure. I am an adult, aware of my strengths and weaknesses, and with the capacity to learn and grow.

I start to speak back to Inner Critic. "Thank you for protecting me, when I was younger, and needed to be as perfect as possible to avoid being punished and shamed. And now, I am an adult, no longer hanging out with people who speak to me that way, so I don't need you to speak to me like that any more either. Everyone makes mistakes. I am still an equal human being, worthy of love and respect. I can now take risks, and be vulnerable. I can show up, and when I make a mistake, or I encounter other opinions, I can learn from them, and grow. My world is expanding."

Inner critic is not finished yet. "But your sins are like filthy rags. You must be holy. Try harder to be pure."

I sigh. "I know that's what we were taught. But really, I don't think that the goal of life is to be perfect. And I don't think being holy is being perfect. I prefer to use the word sacred. All of life is sacred and has intrinsic worth, just as it is, with all its imperfections. I am free to explore, try, experiment and find out. I am free to make mistakes, to own them, and to learn from them. No fear. No shame."

******

In the last chapter, we looked at ways some fear-inducing doctrines can cause anxiety and be used to manipulate our behaviours.

In this chapter, we are going to take a closer look at teaching on holiness. I experienced holiness being defined as purity, perfection and separation. It was used to create both a sense of safety, as the chosen elite, and also an endless striving for moral virtue. The goal of life became to be perfectly good. "Goodness" was defined for us by others. Moral failure was a source of great shame.

The rhetoric went something like this. "Repent of your sins and accept Jesus. Receive his gracious gift of eternal life. Then you must be Holy! Aim for perfection! Be pure! Keep His commandments! We are set apart! We must be different to the world."

I remember passionately singing lyrics like those of Brian Doerksen in Refiner's fire, which implored God to "let me be as gold, pure gold, set apart for you my Master, ready to do your will." I felt privileged to have been born into a family where Bible truths were taught from birth, so all I had to do was accept them to become part of the chosen people, set apart for God and destined for heaven.

Without realising it, my life became about a destination, not the journey. And shame was my travel-companion.

A Chosen People

The idea of holiness as being set apart, or special, chosen people, made me feel I had to know all the answers, without asking any of the questions. I shut down my natural curiosity and did not allow myself to ask difficult questions, because then I risked not belonging. Instead, I was the person who knew The Truth, and needed to evangelise the poor ignorant heathen around me.

It is well-nigh impossible for a child to develop authentic spirituality under these conditions. As we saw in the last chapter, the child's fear of eternal damnation and rejection by their care-givers, will trump their inquisitiveness. Without genuine room to question, true faith does not develop.

There can be the appearance of room for questioning, for example through apologetics. When I was a student at University, I was involved in leading apologetics seeker groups for other students. I thought I was making room for exploration and enquiry. However, I went, as a leader in the group, to present the pre-determined answers to the predictable questions from the agnostics. I was not open to being personally challenged by their questions. I was convinced I already had all the answers and nothing to learn.

It was only much later, at a time of great suffering, that I was cracked open and could see the gaping holes in the faith I had been handed. Only then, could I start the journey of discovering the Divine for myself.

Children do need a frame-work to grow within, that gives them a sense of order and security in the universe. That frame-work also needs to be flexible enough to expand with them as they grow, to lose a pole or two, and to sprout wings. This world desperately needs our children to be able to show up as their unique selves in this world, able to share their wondrous presence and individual gifts with us. We need to learn from them, even as they learn from us.

We do our children no favours, when we present them with a fait accompli. Children are full of curiosity. It is their gift and their natural way of developing and learning. Let them ask their questions and discover their own answers – with a little guidance along the way.

How can we allow them to do this if we hold the view that being holy means being the separate ones who know The Truth, and that not believing this means eternal punishment? Surely there must be other ways of understanding this concept?

What if it is not just us who are chosen, but everybody? What if the path of holiness is not separation but integration, inclusion and welcome?

Perfection

Another definition of holiness is moral perfection. Accepting the belief that being Christian meant trying to be perfect, made admitting mistakes very difficult. If anyone tried to give me constructive feedback, I felt defensive, and shamed. In this kind of environment, it is easier to hide or cover up mistakes, than to learn from them.

I came to realise that my perfectionism was worrying about what other people thought of me, trying to please them and gain acceptance. When I performed well, I gained the approval of my parents and of God. It became the belief that "I am what I do." Brene Brown defines perfectionism from her research as, "a self-destructive and addictive belief system that fuels this primary thought: If I look perfect, live perfectly, work perfectly and do everything perfectly, I can avoid or minimise the painful feelings of shame, judgement and blame."[15]

Perfectionism froze me, because failure meant I felt worthless. It is very hard to be creative, inventive and risk trying something new, when it not working, or criticism, meant I was a failure as a person.

Both being perfect and also making others perceive us as perfect are impossible. Failure is inevitable. When we experience shame as a result of not being perfect, it becomes a vicious, addictive cycle we go round and round, believing that if we can just be more perfect, we will feel OK.

Healthy effort and goals in life need to come from within, not be driven by external forces such as how others think of us. Shame is a cruel master. Shame provokes us to defensive reactions; we hide, cover up, deny, punish or attack.

In contrast, being able to learn from mistakes, grow out of failure, and speak with honesty and vulnerability allows true transformation to take place. The refining fire of mistakes, sin, shadow, suffering and great love mix as alchemy to produce pure gold.

Understanding holiness as a goal is also problematic. It focuses our lives on reaching life after death, paradise or a state of holy perfection. In doing so, it takes our attention away from the here and now. Ordinary everyday things seem irrelevant and unimportant. We lose the sense of the miraculous in the dew on a spider's web, and the magic of a child's laughter.

We can be blind to the holiest of moments in our earthly existence; the lusty cry of the blood-covered new born baby,

---

[15]Brené Brown, *The Gifts of Imperfection: Let Go of Who You Think You're Supposed to Be and Embrace Who You Are.* Hazelden, 2010

flesh of our flesh, and the hush when our loved one takes their final breath and is still. Moments that provoke us to ponder and wonder at this mystery we call life.

Don't you sense the holiness of the instant you connect with Divine love? Do feel the reverence, when we realise that we are in the presence of unconditional love, and can see ourselves as we really are? Do you tingle with awe at the resplendent beauty of pure love, that makes us take off our shoes, and kneel in wonder? How does it feel to encounter the blazing light that shows us our shadow – not to make us cower in fear and self-loathing – but that gives us the clear sight we need to own our weakness and grow towards the light. Have you known the inexplicable comfort, felt when at our lowest, of gentle, warm arms underneath us, sustaining and carrying us until we were back on our feet again, starting to totter forward once more.

The word holiness has so many unhelpful connotations for me, that I prefer to use the word sacred. I think of all living things as having inherent worth, of life itself as sacred. Everyone and everything are included and are worthy of love and respect. The beauty of the natural world speaks of goodness, and is to be looked after. Grandeur and intricate detail can inspire awe and wonder. I appreciate other people most when they show up authentically as their true selves, not as "perfect". And I now give myself the same permission to be vulnerable, to risk making mistakes, to have true curiosity and to encounter the world with an open heart.

And when I have an encounter with someone else who is willing to be vulnerable, someone who does not hide their "warts and all", and gives me the chance to love them, as they really are – boom – that's a holy moment, right there. It brings tears of appreciation to my eyes every time. That kind of courage and love is palpable.

Sometimes asking good questions is more valuable than having the answers. Maybe having a welcoming home is more important than having a clean and tidy one. Peeling back the image and revealing more of your true self to others can create real connection and intimacy. Having a try might be more important than the end result. What if it is all about the journey – not the destination?

What if we do not need a fence of moral rules to keep us feeling superior and safe? What if we can tumble down the wall, and embark on the journey of discovering the sacred in ourselves and each other?

Questions for reflection.

Q1. How would you define holiness?

Q2. What are the holiest moments you have experienced in your life so far?

Q3. What do you feel when you fail?

Q4. Describe how your understanding of coping with failure has changed over time.

Q5. Are there any groups of people you feel you need to keep separate from? Why?

Q6. Who might you include? Learn from? What would that feel like?

Cult of Innocence & forgiveness

The Christianity I grew up in was a shame-based religion in which we craved feeling innocent. As we saw in the last chapter, when the goal is moral purity and perfection, we need to believe that we are clean in order to feel accepted and enough. The problem is we are never perfectly good, no matter how you define purity, or grace. So, we look for a short cut.

I found it really important to come to an understanding of this, in order to comprehend why I had gone along with the oppression of women, the LGBTQ community and others for so long. It helped me to forgive myself, and see a way forward that was actually in line with my own values of inclusion and justice. It helped me grow out of victimhood, and find agency and inner peace.

The short-cut to moral purity is scapegoating and projection. We find a victim to defend and a villain to oppose, and in doing so, feel innocent and righteous ourselves. We are also blind to our own hypocrisy and the harm we are doing in the process.[16]

It makes us feel that we are right, with superior knowledge; we are the ones who believe the Bible, even when our "evil" society and culture rejects "God's teaching" on homosexuality or the role of women. We are on God's side, in His team, and going to heaven. We are holy. We are safe.

But this is not without harmful effects – it causes minimising and denial of the harm done through racism, sexism, oppression of LGBTQ people and the ruthless exploitation

---

[16] For a fuller understanding of the "cult of innocence" read Brian McLaren *Do I Stay Christian?"* Hodder & Stoughton 2022 pp. 171-180

of the environment. When we refuse to see the harm, we become complicit.

I was raised in a Christian community that taught that the oppression of women and of the LGBTQ community was "what the Bible taught" and hence could not be questioned. To accept the equality of women in the clergy or even the home, or allowing gay marriage would have been to reject God. Speaking out against the cultural acceptance of LGBTQ rights became a requisite for being a true Bible believing Christian.

It created a cult of innocence, where the "victim" was "Christian marriage", and the villain was people advocating for women's rights and gay rights. These Christians felt innocent and pure by separating themselves from and opposing these movements.

However, this "innocence" came with a price.

It silenced the voices of the LGBTQ people themselves, denied their lived experience and even told them that they were condemned to hell, causing great harm. This teaching has led to shattering families, addictions, mental illness and deaths by suicide.[17] Similarly, patriarchal teaching has played a large part in silencing women who were suffering, and creating family environments where abusive behaviour could continue unchecked (as I sadly know from first-hand experience).[18] These teachings have caused people to be traumatised.

---

[17] **https://www.thetrevorproject.org/research-briefs/religiosity-and-suicidality-among-lgbtq-youth/** accessed 13.03.2025

[18] **https://www.restored-uk.org/resource/in-churches-too-key-findings/** accessed 13.03.2025

When I was homeschooling our children in Ecuador, I decided it would be good for them to learn about the history of South America, as it is their heritage. When we came to learning about the conquistadores, I was struck by the different way the story is told in the UK textbooks and the Ecuadorean ones. When I was a child, I had been taught that the white settlers saved the ignorant Incas from child-sacrifice, and introduced superior Christian morality. My husband, in Ecuador, had been taught about the white oppressors who violently invaded and plundered their country.

In that moment, as a white woman of privilege, residing as a guest in their country, it caused me to reflect on our history, and what my current attitude and motivation for "serving the local people" really was. I paused and thought about the racism, violence and theft that the people I lived amongst had experienced at the hands of those who professed my religion. Was I still perpetuating any of those harms?

Brian McLaren puts forward an alternative way of dealing with guilt and shame, to that of the cult of innocence. It involves "soberly rethinking the past, facing it without minimising it, grieving over it, feeling the full measure of the pain of the victims, seeking to understand the conditions that prompted the victimisers to do what they did, seeking to address those conditions, healing the wounds, righting the wrongs, changing the systems that protected the wrongdoers, and joining with the victims in a struggle for mutual liberation."[19]

Surely this is the path of Love. It is hard to admit that we have had racist attitudes, or been complicit in the

---

[19] Brian McLaren *Do I Stay Christian?* Hodder & Stoughton 2022 p. 178

oppression of women, or taught things that have allowed domestic abuse to continue in families in our congregations. Are we willing to listen to what the LGBTQ community has to say to us? We need to ask questions about the effect our teaching has had. What role has teaching that the end of the world is nigh, and that humans are to subdue the earth, played in climate change and environmental catastrophe, for example? Facing this will not make us feel morally right and superior. We will no longer be scapegoating someone else as the villain. We will see our own failure.

But it is only through going to these dark places, and grieving over them, that change for the better can be born. It is by shining the light, darkness can be dispelled and true transformation can begin.

I am reminded of a parable Jesus told, of the tax-collector and the pharisee at the altar. The tax-collector prayed, "Have mercy on me, a sinner." The Pharisee prayed, "I thank you God I am not like the tax-collector."[20]

How many of us, on hearing that story condemn the pharisee and then in the same breath say, "Thank God I am not like the pharisee!"?

Or, "Thank God I'm not like those Christians." Or, perhaps, "Thank God I'm not a Christian anymore."

This is just another way to try and feel innocent and good by distancing ourselves from a perceived villain.

Whether or not I choose to keep the label "Christian", what would happen if I say instead, "Have mercy on me," and accepting myself as flawed and also enough, seek to

---

[20] Luke 18 v 9-14

engage in facing the past, healing wounds and participating in the struggle for truth and love?

Truth and reconciliation

Many doctrines of salvation are transactional. They tell us that Jesus death "paid the price for sin", that he was our substitute in the last sin offering satisfying the justice of God, a ransom paid to the devil, or that Jesus was the scapegoat.

The church has had a strong emphasis on feeling shame for sin and looking for who is to blame and punishing them. Western Christian societies developed their justice systems on these principles of law and punishment. Christian families have often raised their children this way, citing verses that state "children obey your parents,"[21] and "spare the roc and spoil the child"[22] as confirmation that they need to require instant obedience and physically chastise their children for breaking the rules.

Perhaps you were raised in this way, and have disciplined your own children in a similar fashion, trying to train them to be good citizens and church members through clear rules and punishment for wrong-doing.

My grandfather was the first education officer in Brixton prison in London. Before that, he taught boys who had been excluded from their local schools. He saw the good in everyone. With great compassion, he offered a way out of the cycle of shame and punishment. He offered an opportunity to learn and grow and change, without violence.

I think South Africa was one of the first countries to do this on a large scale, with the Truth and Reconciliation project,

---

[21] Ephesians 6 v 1

[22] Proverbs 13 v 24

run by Nelson Mandela and Desmond Tutu. It aimed to provide restorative justice. Victims were invited to give statements about their experiences, and perpetrators could also give testimony and request amnesty from prosecution. The organisers were seeking a way to transition from apartheid without perpetuating the cycle of violence and revenge, and also without minimising the suffering of the victims.[23]

Forgiveness can be weaponised. Jesus' death – however you understand it – should not be used to minimise pain, silence victims or coerce them into staying in dangerous or damaging environments. We need to be very careful about what we teach regarding forgiveness to victims, and not give them harmful messages.

A person who is experiencing abuse from their partner does not need to be told to forgive seventy times seven[24], and to stay in the relationship. They need to be helped to safety.

Someone who experienced abuse from their parent in childhood, and chooses to be estranged from them as an adult for their own wellbeing, does not need to be told to forgive. Forgiveness and reconciliation are two different things.

People are more important than institutions and doctrines.

Forgiveness cannot be rushed. "I forgive you" is a process, not a sentence. Forgiveness burns in our chest, sweats tears of anguish, wriggles and squirms, silently screams in fear, rages against the injustice of it all, and brings inner peace.

---

[23] You can read more about it here **https://www.justice.gov.za/trc/**

[24] Matthew 18 v 22

Forgiveness is not easy. It cannot be required or imposed by another person or institution. It does not sweep under the carpet, cover up or protect the perpetrator. It does not let the offender off the hook.

Wherever I encounter forgiveness, there seems to be a consensus that forgiveness is for the benefit of the victim, not the perpetrator. It gifts inner freedom from hate, chronic anger and resentment. It sets the victim free to live their life in peace.

Forgiving yourself is the most important – and the most difficult.

In The Book of Forgiving by Desmond and Mpho Tutu[25], they describe a fourfold path to forgiveness, born out of their experience of apartheid, the murder of a close friend and the truth and reconciliation project in South Africa.

The first two steps involve admitting the wrong, and the harm it did, including feeling the anguish it caused. These steps cannot be glossed over. We cannot pay lip service to forgiveness – saying we forgive intellectually because it is what is expected of us by our moral code or religion.

Sometimes, not telling the story of what happened, and naming the harm it caused goes so far as covering up the wrong to protect the offender. Other times, we cannot admit to ourselves something we have done, or our belief that a wrong was our fault.

Shining a light on what is hiding in the shadow allows it to be spoken, witnessed and heard. It grants the opportunity

---

[25] Desmond and Mpho Tutu *The Book of Forgiving: The Fourfold Path for Healing Ourselves and Our World* HarperCollins 2014 I listened to this on audible and found it an excellent way to be lead through the suggested exercises.

for growth and change. True transformation cannot occur while wrongs remain unspoken, boxed up or buried.

The third step is to ask for and grant forgiveness. There are a few things to note here. Forgiving someone does not require them to ask for forgiveness. A person can deny a wrong completely, and the victim can still forgive them. Forgiveness is for the benefit of the victim.

Similarly, forgiving yourself does not depend on anyone else forgiving you.

Also, forgiveness does not mean justice is not also sought or served, or that the wrong does not matter. Consequences may well still follow. Forgiveness cannot bring the dead to life, restore a lost childhood, or erase the memories that have caused a loss of trust. Forgiveness is inner work, that brings inner tranquillity to troubled waters.

I do not find forgiveness to be a virtue someone can be exhorted to exercise. Nor do I find it to be some kind of transaction.

I meet forgiveness as an invitation to let go of the inner destructiveness of hate. I find it to be an invitation to step into the flow of love again; to love myself and recognise that common humanity in all of us.

This third step is based on empathy. It is recognising that intrinsic worth as human beings in all of us, that sacredness and woundedness of the human soul.

In their book, the Tutus describe an exercise where they invite the reader to write the wrongs of a person in the sand on a beach, and their loving actions on a rock. The sea comes in and washes away the wrongs. The love remains.

We can do the same for ourselves. We are just as human as everyone else. We are *only* human; in that we too wrong others and ourselves. We are *also* human; in that we share the same intrinsic value and worth. We too are the beloved. I find that the more I am able to forgive my own imperfections, and come to accept myself as I am, the more I can forgive and accept others, warts and all.

A most powerful paragraph in the book The Choice by Edith Eger[26], an Auschwitz survivor, is when she returns to Auschwitz years later, and recalls standing in the line on their entry to the camp. The guard asked her if her mother was her mother, or her sister. She replied, "My Mother." Those words condemned her mother to instant death in the gas chambers, as only younger women were being kept alive. Telling that story to her own, now adult daughter, allows Edith to forgive herself, and allows deeper healing of her terrible trauma.

All the while we harbour hate towards ourselves for our real or perceived failings, we project this anger and dysfunction on to our loved ones around us. Forgiving ourselves, accepting our own humanity, sets us free to live imperfectly, with joy. It opens up that accepting space for others.

The fourth step is renewing or releasing the relationship. All too often, it is assumed that forgiveness equals reconciliation. Many times, it does. It can be a very necessary part of any healthy relationship and happen over and over again.

When this is the case, boundaries need to be set going forward. The relationship does not go back to how it was before. It moves on to something new. Forgiving a betrayal is not a carte blanche to accept the same behaviours all over

---

[26] Edith Eger *The Choice* Penguin Audio 2017 – This is well worth a read/listen. The amazing account of her journey through hell, to freedom and healing

again. Both parties need to clearly express their intentions and limits going forward. Boundaries are a healthy expression of "the distance at which I can love you and love me simultaneously." To quote Prentis Hemphill. Boundaries can also evolve over time.

However, there are times when we choose not to renew a relationship. That does not mean we have not forgiven. It is a perfectly legitimate choice to make. Sometimes it is a very necessary expression of self-care and self-protection – for example for people escaping domestic abuse, repeated betrayals, or for survivors of childhood abuse. There is no need to feel guilty if that is your choice with a certain person or people.

And with great compassion I write that sometimes releasing the relationship is the choice we want to make, but circumstances prevent it. For example, when parenting or care-giving responsibilities are shared with the perpetrator. This is a very difficult and often painful path to walk. It requires firm boundaries to be set, and often mediators who are willing to step in and help. The cycle of forgiveness will need to be practiced over and over again. I see and hear your anguish. Be very kind to yourself.

Shine the light and grow

I remember sitting with a group of women and my own daughters in the kitchen of a family member in Ecuador. A little boy went to pull the saucepans off the shelf *again*, after his mum had repeatedly told him not to. She went to smack him in punishment. We were visiting from Scotland at the time, and I made the comment that in Scotland it was now illegal for us to physically punish our children. It was now regarded as assault, just as it would be if we hit an adult.

The young mother paused, and then commented that yes, she did not enjoy hitting her son. With genuine curiosity and desire to learn something new, she asked what parents did instead to correct and teach their children. Other mothers in the room, including myself, started contributing their regrets in how they had chastised their children in the past. Our children were there listening to this conversation. And then we started talking about healthier ways of teaching our children, at different ages and stages, and how we are all learning as we go along.

Mothers were able to share how, so often, they were angry with their children, when the real problem was that they were worrying about their relationship with their partner, or money, or something else, and had very little patience as a result. It opened up space where the adults could support each other and ask for help when needed. And the children could hear that there was nothing wrong with them.

As I, and my daughters, listened to this conversation, and contributed, without judgement or shame, my heart felt wide open and full of hope. All of us, the youngsters included, were learning it is good to shine the light on the shadows so that we can learn and grow. We were teaching ourselves and our children, that we are all in a constant process of making mistakes and learning from them. No one in that room claimed to be the perfect parent; not the grannies nor the young mums, not the white nor the brown skinned, not the rich nor the poor, not the catholic nor the protestant nor the agnostic. We were all human, capable of learning from and supporting each other. And it was OK for our children to make mistakes, need support and grow too.

What if the cross is about ending punishment? What if it is about non-violence? What if it is about ending shame, being vulnerable and courageous, and unconditional love? What do you think?

Questions for reflection.

Q1. Can you think of a time when you were blamed, shamed and punished? What did that feel like? What did it achieve?

Q2. Can you think of a time when you were in an environment with a growth mindset, where mistakes were learnt from without shame? What did that feel like? What did it achieve?

Q3. Have you been in a church that taught doctrines as essential to the gospel, that you now disagree with? What were they? What do you think now?

Q4. What do you think of the "cult of innocence" theory, as Brian Mclaren calls it? Have you experienced this, or seen it at work? Can you give an example?

Q5. Have you experienced or seen forgiveness being weaponised? What happened?

Q6. How do you understand forgiveness?

Q7. How do you understand the cross and salvation? Has that changed for you?

Authority

The family and religion that I was brought up in was very authoritarian. Authority was male.

Children and women obeyed and deferred to male authority. God was male and the ultimate authority. In summary, God's instruction was "obey the male head of your house and obey the male leaders of your church, and then you will be obeying God."

Children had to obey their parents, because this was the first commandment with a promise[27]. The promise was that the child would then have long life, which would go well.

Wives had to submit to their husbands. This was said to mean that the husband had authority over his wife, and his children. Wives promised to obey their husbands in their marriage vows. Children watched this play out. The children were to obey, or they were punished. They watched their mothers obeying their fathers. Wives had to ask any theological questions they might have of their husbands, who was especially recognised as the spiritual authority in the Christian family. In church, women served the tea, cared for the children, and sang, while the men stood at the front and preached, prayed aloud and told everyone else how they should behave, and the way to God.

Depending on the denomination, women and girls were told how long they might have their hair, to wear a covering on their head to church as a sign of submission and not to wear trousers.

When women objected to this unequal treatment, mental gymnastics were employed to justify why it was really fine.

---

[27] Ephesians 6 v 1-4

This included being told it was because Eve was the one deceived, not Adam. And that actually it was a huge responsibility for the man, because ultimately, he was the one who had to make the decisions for everyone else. And that, as this was a mandate from God, it did not matter if the man took bad decisions, as God would honour them and bless them regardless, simply because God's order of things was being obeyed. And that in contrast, if the woman disagreed and asserted herself, and made a decision for the family, even if it was a good one, then God would not bless the family. And that women were really privileged in all of this, because all they had to do was respect their husband and church leaders. The men had to sacrifice themselves for the women. They were the ones who had the hard role to play.

Women sacrificing their authentic needs and desires, women suppressing and agreeing not to use their God-given talents and abilities, women sacrificing their voice, power and agency was minimised and normalised. After all, this was the essence of "Biblical womanhood" wasn't it? Deny yourself, sacrifice, and be selfless.

Now, in a home and congregation where the men believed the women to be equal, and loved them such that they gave equal importance to their needs and views, this could play out without abuse of power or women losing their voice. But even in these healthier households and churches, I venture there are women who do not develop and contribute gifts and talents they possess, because they believe it is not part of their role. I imagine everyone loses out when the contribution a person is permitted to make remains defined by gender, and a gendered power structure.

More concerningly, wherever there is a power dynamic, such as patriarchal authority, the risk of abuses such as gender-based violence and coercive control is high.

Let's explore what happens when the children are indoctrinated and disempowered, and the women are programmed to defer to authority, such that they cannot then function as autonomous human beings in the world. What happens when this authoritarian view of life leads to power being misused, coercion and control being exerted over women, children and congregations? What happens when a man with a narcissistic personality takes control of a family or congregation?

Passive Women

A family can operate believing in mutual submission and equality, and the children grow witnessing honest debate, mutual compromise, respect for different opinions, and roles not being defined on the basis of gender alone. Children are listened to, and responded to. Demands made of them are in keeping with their age, stage and ability. They are allowed to challenge their parents and their authority sometimes, and are taught to question other adults respectfully.

Harmful dynamics creep in, as the spectrum shifts to blind obedience. This can occur in families where there is no ill intent. It is not deliberate control of others. It comes from a genuine place of fear. We can have compassion for such parents, and also see the harm it has done and the need to break the cycle of this continuing into future generations.

Imagine two parents who were raised in a conservative church themselves, and taught to fear God, hell, the end of the world and punishment, as we discussed in previous chapters. They believe that in order to please God, He must be obeyed. Obeying God means the man is in charge, making the decisions, and the wife submits at home and in church, serving selflessly. Obeying God means the children are compliant, obedient and bring no shame on the family.

If the children rebel, the man risks losing his status as a leader in the church[28].

As soon as reputation starts becoming more important than the well-being of individuals, there is likely harm being done. Those who are under authority will not be able to express their questions, experiment, or try a different way of doing things, because the potential for shame and rejection is too great. If they do beg to differ, they will be labelled a rebel or black sheep or spoken of as a backslider.

Children need their attachment to their care-givers to survive. Their automatic response to threat will be to suppress their own needs, emotions and questions, and develop a trauma response, such as fawn (people pleasing) or freeze (passivity). When they see this modelled by their mother, they are likely to copy her example.

Sometimes the mother will be very authoritarian herself, perhaps especially when her husband is out. She might only know how to be a strict disciplinarian. Or she might take out her own frustration and worries on the children. She may be suffering abuse and be acting out of a trauma response herself.

A wife who believes that this is God's order of things, and that she should submit, may collude with the idea that the man is more important, his role more demanding, his reputation to be protected. She may believe she is giving a good example to her daughters of how to be a good Christian wife. She may feel trapped, without alternative, as to push back against this would mean losing all that is precious to her.

---

[28] 1 Timothy 3

Without intending to, harm can be done by the enactment of these ideas and roles. Women and girls especially, can become adults who automatically defer to authority, with a sense of fear, and lack the ability to critically question authority figures. This places them in a dangerous position, vulnerable to being taken advantage of. Not to mention the way everyone loses out when someone does not develop the capacity to think for themselves and put forward their own ideas and opinions. We all miss out when someone does not develop and contribute their own gifts and talents to our world.

Girls raised in this way can end up very passive. When asserting yourself earns negative feedback or disapproval, the child learns to only respond to the cues they receive, never to assert their own needs or wants. They are also often anxious, and/or anxious to please. This is a very limiting cocktail.

If this goes on for a long time, and is reinforced over time, the child may never learn to recognise their own needs and wants and preferences. If the child is taught that it is God's will that they blindly obey their parents, and that girls must submit to male authority, (or authority in general), this can become an underlying limiting belief. Asserting themselves then feels shameful and wrong.

Add to the mix the teaching that Christians should surrender to God: that God's will should become their will, that they should surrender their own desires and only desire what God wants. This is the perfect recipe for producing passive people with an external locus of control.

Passive people tend to keep quiet, to hide their true feelings, to observe and respond, rather than initiating conversation or suggesting ideas. They are unlikely to venture true opinions, or to take the lead. They have learnt that it is safer to be small, unnoticed and self-effacing. It is safer to go with the majority, or do as they are told. They may even believe it is wrong to be noticed or to use their talents, or for example to lead in church, because they are female.

Having an external locus of control means believing outside factors determine what happens to you in life. So, a passive person with an external locus of control might say, "God determines my future, all I can do is go along with what the Bible says, and the rest is in God's hands." This person feels they have very little control and say over what happens to them. They are unlikely to actively engage in life. When they experience failure or disappointment, they shrug and say it was not meant to be, or that it was not God's will. It is very hard for them to make meaningful changes in their lives, because they believe their effort will be in vain. It is all pre-determined.

In contrast, a person with an internal locus of control believes that their own decisions and actions directly influence their own successes and future. They take responsibility for their own actions, and believe that their own hard work enables them to achieve success. When they experience failure or disappointment, they use it as an opportunity to learn and grow. They successfully make meaningful changes in their lives, because they believe their effort will bring results.

Christian women, who believe they should submit, obey, deny themselves and sacrifice themselves, have an external locus of control. Indeed, they instinctively believe having an internal locus of control is sinful. They believe they should cast themselves on the goodwill of God and the men appointed to rule over them, and surrender all control over their own lives. They totally lack agency.

Agercy is the sense of control that you feel in your life, your capacity to influence your own thoughts and behaviour, and have faith in your ability to handle a wide range of tasks and situations. For a woman who has been conditioned to believe having agency is sinful, it can be a long road to come to the point where she gives herself permission to claim her own right to have independent thoughts, decide how she is going to behave in any given circumstance, and develop her ability to handle all kinds of different tasks and situations.

Until she gives herself that permission, she will be a rudderless ship, blown here and there by whichever wind is buffeting her.

If you recognise yourself here, and you feel you need Biblical permission to see things differently, have a read of Ephesians 4 v 14-16. It is talking about what happens when everyone uses their gifts to build each other up. "Then we will no longer be immature like children. We won't be tossed and blown about by every wind of new teaching. We will not be influenced when people try to trick us with lies so clever they sound like the truth. Instead, we will speak the truth in love, growing in every way more and more like Christ, who is the head of his body, the church... As each part does its own special work, it helps the other parts grow, so that the whole body is healthy and growing and full of love."[29]

You have permission to be healthy and growing and full of love. This includes psychological and emotional health, and a healthy sense of self and self-determination.

Coercive Control and Gender Based Violence

Teaching men that they have an automatic right to lead and make decisions simply because of their Y chromosome has

---

[29] Ephesians 4 v 14-16

caused great harm. It is easy to see why male entitlement develops. Men raised in such a way can believe that they have a God-given right to certain privileges. They can develop the belief that they are superior. They may enjoy the power and control handed to them, develop an inflated sense of self-importance and crave the admiration and praise they receive for performing public acts such as preaching or leading services. With these characteristics, you have the makings of a narcissist. Patriarchal leadership structures in churches and families play into their hands.

These men are generally publicly admired, with a great reputation and ability to impress and charm others. Behind closed doors, in their own families, or with people they have power over in the church, it is a different story. Mix them together with the passive, submissive wife or congregant, and you have the classic power imbalance where abuse, coercive control and high-control religion can prosper.

When the perpetrator emotionally, verbally, physically or sexually abuses their partner and/or children, the victims think they deserve it, because they are not obeying or submitting well enough. The manipulation and gas-lighting convince them of their lack of worth. They think that the abusive behaviour is normal and expected. They minimise their negative feelings about it and feel it is wrong of them to feel upset. They believe they should be selfless and that this means their feelings are unimportant. They fear it would be useless to speak up anyway, because no one would believe them, or they would be told to submit more, so that they can "win round their partner for the gospel."

If you are struggling to understand how this plays out, let's look at an example. Monica grew up in a Christian home. It was quite a protected childhood. She went to school, but most of her spare time was spent at home or at church. Her father was an authoritarian head of the home. He was a leader in their local church and respected in the community. He set out the rules for his family very clearly and expected instant obedience from his children. Monica felt quite afraid of him. If she stepped out of line she was smacked, or put into silence. So, she did the very best she could to obey without question.

Generally, home felt more relaxed when her father was out at work. Her mother cooked and cleaned and looked after the children. She was really very shy and did not go out, except to go to church. Monica heard her father call her mother "stupid" and "lazy" a lot. He expected a hot meal on the table as soon as he came in, and that the children would be quiet, clean and toys put away. Monica saw her mother cry sometimes, when her father had put her into silent treatment for disrespecting him. Her mother never took them out for a treat, or went to visit friends, because her father monitored the mileage in the car, and would notice if it had been driven further than school and back. He also demanded receipts for every purchase, so controlled every penny that was spent. He also went through the phone bill, so there was no way to make a phone call without his knowledge and approval.

All of this felt normal to Monica, because it was all she had ever known. She rarely visited other people's houses, and did not know how things were done in their homes. She believed this was what the man being head of the household meant. She believed that to be good and accepted by God, she needed to obey. She felt upset with her mother if she resisted her father's control. Her mother should be obeying without question too. If her father got angry with her mother, it felt like it was her mother's fault.

When Monica grew up, she fell in love and married. At first, she loved the attention and the gifts from her husband. Very soon, however, he started hitting her when she upset him.

However hard she tried; she seemed unable to please him and not provoke him to anger. And he demanded sex more than once a day. She wanted to obey and please him, so why did she feel so used? She started to feel very depressed and anxious. Who could she speak to about this? She tried a Christian counsellor, but they kept speaking about learning to submit. They urged her to pray harder for her husband. She felt it was all her fault. She should have more faith. She deserved to be treated this way. The most important thing was to keep the marriage together, as a good Christian witness to the world.

I hope you can see how distorted all this has become, but that for someone who is stuck in it, with such ingrained ideas about what being the head of the house and submission means, they end up trapped in abuse. Tragically, all too often Christian counselling and pastoral advice has played into the hands of the abuser and utterly failed to defend and liberate the victim.

There are several factors at play here, and I hope this book is giving you permission to question how you understand many of these teachings. For the purposes of this chapter, we are going to concentrate on the role gender-based authority plays.

Some people who escape an abusive home like this walk away from faith completely. The treatment they have experienced is too far removed from Love, and the church too complicit in protecting the perpetrators.

Others, want to hold on to faith in a God of Love, but need to find a safe way to do so, which does not place them in danger of being controlled and manipulated and harmed once again.

This a very individual journey, and will need many different kinds of support along the way. If you would like to find some support after experiencing domestic abuse in a Christian context, I recommend the charity Restored[30] in the UK. All I would like to offer here is to point out how Jesus treated women. Take a moment to pause and reflect on this quote from Dorothy L Sayers.

"Perhaps it is no wonder that the women were first at the Cradle and last at the Cross. They had never known a man like this Man - there never has been such another. A prophet and teacher who never nagged at them, never flattered or coaxed or patronised; who never made arch jokes about them, never treated them either as "The women, God help us!" or "The ladies, God bless them!"; who rebuked without querulousness and praised without condescension; who took their questions and arguments seriously; who never mapped out their sphere for them, never urged them to be feminine or jeered at them for being female; who had no axe to grind and no uneasy male dignity to defend; who took them as he found them and was completely unself-conscious. There is no act, no sermon, no parable in the whole Gospel that borrows its pungency from female perversity; nobody could possibly guess from the words and deeds of Jesus that there was anything "funny" about woman's nature."[31]

If you want to, what kind of relationship could you have with this Jesus?

Narcissistic Abuse in Church

---

[30] **https://www.restored-uk.org/**

[31] Dorcthy L. Sayers, *Are Women Human? Penetrating, Sensible and Witty Essays on the Role of Women in Society* William B. Eerdmans Publishing Company 1995

If you read the news at all, you will be familiar with recent scandals regarding some famous church leaders. These abuses of power happen frequently too in smaller congregations and groups. Church leadership can be very appealing for those who have a narcissistic personality, because it plays into their beliefs that they are special, that they know the truth, that they are superior to others and entitled to certain privileges.

Such beliefs can be overt, expressed as knowing the truth about God, being part of *the* group that is going to heaven, being entitled to lead because they are male, etc. Other times, they can be more covert, appearing as charismatic, caring, winsome personalities in public, but then creating a subculture, for example amongst their leadership team, where they abuse their power to gain certain privileges and manipulate people into doing things they never wanted to go along with. This can include sexual abuse and physical violence.

Where there is a narcissist, there are always people who collude. These people derive certain benefits from being "on the side" of the narcissist, and assist them, sometimes unwittingly, in gaslighting, twisting the truth, and asserting certain beliefs with the goal of maintaining control over other people. They will also not believe victims when they start to speak out about the abuses that are occurring, and defend the institution of the church, the leader themself, and attempt to silence the victims.

Christians who have been raised to blindly obey and accept the authority of their spiritual leaders are vulnerable to being taken in by these power-hungry leaders, who are, in reality, wolves dressed in sheep's clothing.

The sense of betrayal, and shock at being taken in by such a person can be immense, and need skilled help to unravel.

We all need to increase our awareness of these dynamics and be on the watch for them. We all need to trust our own instincts about a person or leadership team. We need to be able to identify toxic dynamics and call them out. We need to examine what has gone wrong in the past and learn from it. We need to change our ideas, beliefs and practices around leadership and improve safeguarding further. We can all be part of doing it differently.

Healing from abuse of power

There are other ways of understanding how family relationships work. There are different interpretations of what headship means and what authority is given to whom and for what purpose. You do not have to simply accept what you were given. There are other stories than the fall of Eve, and indeed varying ways of understanding that story. You can explore, experiment and decide for yourself. Here are some ideas to get you going.

The story of Eve taking the fruit and eating it, and her subsequent cursing, has been told to us as the story that defines the role and subjugation of women ever since. What about the other stories?

What about the creation story, where the woman was declared very good? Have you claimed your inherent goodness as a blessing to this world yet? Have you thought about your miraculous ability to bring forth new life on earth? Have you recognised your unique gifts and abilities that you can use to nurture, protect and nourish your corner of the planet and your community?

How about the story of Mary, mother of Jesus, told by angel Gabriel, when she was just a young girl, that she was to bear the son of God. She said "yes", even though she knew others would think it all a scandal and sinful. Whose authority was she under there? Did she run to the priest, or her father for permission or advice? Not that we know of. She recognised her own inner authority. She believed in her own ability to recognise the voice of God, and courageously trusted her own response.

Spiritual authority does not come from being born a certain gender, or into a certain system. It comes from recognising an authentic message and witnessing the power of that path to transform. It is something we can all develop, through spiritual practices which teach us to listen within, such as lectio divina, meditation, silence, solitude, nature and Ignatian prayer of examen. Our bodies do not lie. When we stop for long enough and regularly enough to listen, we find have this wisdom and authority within us already. We need to learn to obey our own deepest voices.

As more people do this, the authority of the Bible or God is not lessened, but increased, because we will have more people able to offer true interpretations and lived spiritual experiences. We will have more people seeing well through the lens of love and able to instruct and encourage each other.

We also see this spiritual authority in people who have lived the talk. These are the people who have suffered, and experienced transformation, coming out the other side with more freedom, joy and a contagious appreciation of life itself. It is often those wounds which we have allowed to transform us as they heal, which give us each the place where we can make our greatest contribution to the journeys of others.

Going through the process of transformation, finding the way back to unleashing true self can be very hard. It takes a lot of courage, because it is so fear-inducing: fear of judgement and criticism, fear of failure, fear of an unpleasant reaction, fear of not being enough.

I think I found it possible to start the journey by noticing how much I appreciate it when I meet other people who gently and confidently show up as themselves. These people know they are unique, special, and that they have something only they can contribute to life. They also know we live in a world of abundance – that every single one of us is special and has that wonderful, individual gift to give.

They remain respectful of others. They believe in themselves and that they have valid opinions to offer and dreams to bring to life.

They rejoice when others shine and offer their artistry, skill and love.

Having the courage to remove the mask, and let others see your true self requires a constellation of actions. First, we need to put limiting beliefs and roles aside, and be willing to feel the vulnerability and shame that will surface. We need to learn to accept both comfortable and uncomfortable emotions, and simply let them be felt.

We also need to get in touch with our true self, through contemplation, "just being" exercises, and learning to listen to our bodies. Our minds are so easily manipulated. As we practice, we learn to recognise that inner truth, our own inner spiritual authority.

Oftentimes, a creative outlet will help the process. This helps explore emotions and process them. What it is exactly is different for each person. It may be journalling, poetry, art, textiles, music, dance, or something else. Creativity helps us learn to explore, try, express and start to dream our own dreams. Doing some work on being assertive can also help. We grow in taking responsibility for ourselves, and living as an equal human being on this planet. We develop our inner locus of control, and belief that we can make a difference, learn from mistakes and make decisions about our own futures.

And then, we get really brave! It is time to share an opinion! Go do that presentation, or share your creative work with someone. The moment has come to start making eye contact with people you meet. Ask for what you need. Take the initiative in greeting people in a gathering. Ask the questions in a conversation. Participate in the meeting. Think of something you would really love to do, and then plan, organise and do it. Learn a new skill. Tell someone your dream, and before long take the first small step towards it. Lead yourself. Know that you are quite capable of this. Gather friends who will cheer you on!

And if that last paragraph has given you a panic attack – remember you don't have to do this all at once. Start with those things that are building your self-confidence and self-worth in private. There is no time scale set for this.

Nonetheless, the world would love to see you take up some space. When your smile lights up your eyes, those you meet each day will be blessed. You are allowed to have emotions, needs, wants and dreams. You are permitted to make mistakes and have questions. You are a unique presence in this world. You belong. You are welcome, just as you are.

Questions for reflection.

Q1. What authority structures did you experience as a child? How did these shape you?

Q2. What do you think healthy family relationships look like?

Q3. What do you think healthy church leadership looks like?

Q4. Are you passive, submissive and obedient? How has that served you? How has it harmed you?

Q5. Is your locus of control external or internal? What beliefs contribute to that?

Q6. Have you tried contemplative spiritual practices such as lectio divina, prayer of examen or meditation of some kind? What do you think about these? Is there something else that helps you listen to your inner voice?

Q7. What is your next step towards taking responsibility for yourself, developing your agency and showing up in the world more fully?

Purity Culture

I grew up in evangelical Christian circles in the UK, in the 1980s and 90s, with a very strict moral purity code around sexuality. It was the era of books such as "I kissed dating goodbye" by Joshua Harris (who has since withdrawn it from publication) and Passion and Purity by Elizabeth Elliot. Fathers in the USA were giving purity rings to their daughters, as they pledged to remain virgins until their marriage day. Although it was not stated in these words, what follows is the message I received.

"As a girl, your virginity is one of the most precious things about you. Once you have lost it, you can never get it back, and you will never be pure again. You must only ever give yourself to one man. If you have sex with more than one person, it is like sticky tape, that becomes less sticky each time you peel it off. Once you have slept with one man, you are one flesh, you belong to him. You will never be able to form an intimate connection with someone else.

It is your responsibility to guard your virginity. Men are sexual animals. They cannot control themselves. You must not dress in an immodest manner. If you do, and it leads to a man or boy sexually assaulting you, it is your fault. When you are going out with a boy, it is the girl who has to keep the boundaries on the physical relationship. Boys are incapable of stopping once they are aroused. The girl needs to keep the brakes on. If you end up having sex with a boy before marriage, it is your fault for not saying "no" early enough, even if you say "no" part way through and he forces you.

Having sex before marriage is wicked. It is a deeply shameful thing to do. If you do this, you will bring shame on yourself, your family and your church community. It is a terrible witness to the world. God will be angry with you. You can ask for forgiveness, and it will of course be given, but you will forever be known as a fallen, disgraced woman. If you are employed in Christian work, you are likely to lose your job.

And you will have to live with the consequences. If you get pregnant, it is your own fault and you will have to bring up that child. Abortion is murder and evil. You will need to marry the man ASAP to mitigate the shame and damage to your reputation, and the witness of the Christian church. If you get a STD, you will be damaged forever. You might die of AIDS. You should not ask about using condoms or other methods of contraception to protect yourself, because you absolutely should abstain until marriage. Therefore, there is no need for you to know about other methods of protection.

You must only go out with and marry Christians, otherwise you will be unequally yoked. If you date or marry a non-Christian, and anything bad happens to you, it is your own fault for disobeying this rule. If you do marry a Christian, then it is guaranteed that your life will be happy and God will bless your home.

Sex was created by God and is good. As soon as you are married, you must have lots of it! You must keep your husband satisfied sexually. Men need lots of sex, otherwise they will have an affair, or look at porn. Once you are married, your body belongs to your husband. You must never say "no" when he asks for sex. You must submit to your husband and his desires. If you have honoured God, by waiting for marriage to have sex, and have married a Christian man, God will honour you. Your marriage will be wonderful and you will be happy ever after.

Hand your love life over to God. Trust Him to find you that perfect partner. Maybe you are called to be single, which is more Holy. You must wait on God, not actively hunt for a marriage partner."

*****

I would like to name the messages given here, and the harm they do.

Women are objectified as sexual objects. "Keeping sexual intercourse in its proper place" is made more important than the people involved and the quality of the relationship. Women, and their bodies are made into the property of men, to be available to be used by men whenever he desires. Women who live this reality end up feeling used, possessed, and of little worth.

Girls' bodies are sexualised. Teaching a girl that she should dress modestly so that boys do not lust after her, places the responsibility for the boy's thoughts and behaviours on her shoulders. Boys learn to focus on the girl's body, rather than learning to speak to her and respect her as a whole human being. This leads to girls wrongfully feeling shame towards their bodies and sexuality, and boys failing to value girls as people worthy of equal respect.

A woman's value/worth depends on her virginity/purity. She knows this to be true by the consequences of failing to remain a virgin until her wedding day. She knows this will invoke shame, and that others will look down on her as a "fallen" woman. A pregnancy that occurs outside of matrimony will be a crisis. She also sees that the men involved rarely face the same censure. They may receive a rap on the knuckles, but their worth is unaffected. "It is men's nature after all, isn't it?" people say. Women who have been raised with this teaching, who are not virgins on their wedding day, often report then feeling like they are used goods, and believing that their marriage will never be a success because of their sin and that they can never enjoy marital sex for the guilt they carry.

A rape-culture is created. While dating, it is the girl's fault if a man assaults her. When married, she has no right to say "no". This leads to women and girls being raped and assaulted on dates and in their own homes. The younger generation find it shocking that marital rape was not criminalised until the 1990s in many western Christian nations, including the UK. Until then, the "I do" on the wedding day was considered consent for the rest of the marriage no matter what.

To this day, some Christian counsellors and pastors who subscribe to purity culture teaching still respond to victims of sexual assault with judgement instead of support. Such counsellors tell young women who have been raped by their boyfriends that they are partly to blame, and focus on the sin of sex outside marriage, shaming the victim, instead of recognising the aggression and trauma, and reporting the crime. Such pastors tell women who report marital rape that there is no such thing, and that they are at fault for not submitting. They counsel women in coercive, controlling and abusive relationships to stay, prolonging the suffering and trauma. There are women who are courageously reporting the crimes committed against them in the past twenty years, who then find those they sought counsel from at the time refuse to make statements to the police to corroborate their evidence.

Other women, brainwashed into believing that their role is to submit to their husband's sexual desires, and totally lacking in education about consent and sexual offenses, continue to live this reality day by day, totally unaware that what they are enduring is sexual coercion, assault and rape. As speaking about intimate relationships is still relatively taboo in these Christian circles, she may never share her experience with her close friends or family, or do so only to be told that is what submitting in marriage means. She may feel ashamed for not wanting his advances, or feel she is inadequate or not normal. She may have so little voice that she never tells her husband "No", or what she likes and dislikes. The trauma inflicted on her by repeated unwanted sexual intercourse or sexual acts she finds repulsive or painful, will lead to trauma responses such as dissociation, depression and anxiety.

Purity culture teaching causes sex to become associated with shame. Shame is feeling you are not enough. Being a virgin on your wedding day has become synonymous with being a good Christian and a good Christian witness. Failing to meet that standard – or in more conservative circles even kissing before marriage – was made into a shameful thing, whereby women especially would feel they were then second-class wives, or fear they had already irrevocably bonded themselves to a previous partner through having had intercourse with them. Sometimes, even women who experienced sexual abuse or rape prior to marriage, because they were taught that sex bonded them to a partner for life, and left them less able to then bond to a new partner, felt they were damaged goods, and that they would never be good enough for their husband.

Becoming pregnant outside of marriage carries stigma still in these Christian circles. It is such a public disgrace. Women can be asked to meet the elders to confess, or to give a public confession to the congregation, in order to be allowed to continue to receive Holy Communion for example. Women in Christian ministry who become pregnant outside of marriage will often be expected to resign their job. They are met with judgement and punishment. Does anyone enquire as to the circumstances leading up to these "moral failures" and offer compassionate support? In my experience, not as often as you might like to think.[32]

The moral failure of sexual sins is seen to be so bad that it can lead to a woman being rejected by her community. Sexual behaviour has become a gate-keeper for admission and expulsion from the church or communion table. I find this focus on sex outside marriage especially problematic, because it is blinkered to other arguably more harmful behaviours. It is all about being seen to be holy and different from the secular world, about having higher moral standards and supporting a Christian model for family life. It places more value on the institution of marriage than the people within it. It seeks to control people's behaviour, rather than facilitate real transformation. It ignores, is blind to, or even promotes the surely more harmful date and marital rape culture that I discussed above.

Purity culture teaches that women and girls must be passive and submissive. As we saw in the previous chapter, this leads to a loss of contributions from women, a lack of agency and voice. It places women in a disempowered, vulnerable position.

These teachings can then lead to the idea that if the husband is unfaithful or has a sex addiction, it is the woman's fault for not giving him enough sex. Books such as "The Power of a Praying Wife"[33] and films such as "War Room"[34], encourage women to pray and pray endlessly for

---

[32] You can read about people's experiences in the comments sections on baremarriage.com blog

[33] Stormie Omartian *The Power of a Praying Wife* Harvest House Publishers 2014

[34] Kendrick Brothers Productions *The War Room* 2015

their straying spouse, in effect placing the responsibility for the man changing on the wife's shoulders and blocking her exit route. Women who take this advice stay for years in dysfunctional, damaging relationships and emerge with betrayal trauma.

In purity culture, women are expected to stop themselves from having intercourse, when aroused, during dating, and then suddenly switch to wanting sex whenever the man does as soon as they are married. (This is called obligation sex). This causes a higher incidence of vaginismus in Christian women with these beliefs compared to those who do not.[35] The harm caused by the duty sex message has been found to be comparable to the trauma caused in victims of sexual assault and rape. This makes sense, because in both cases the victims lack agency and autonomy over their own bodies and sexuality. Instead, the other person holds the power and control.

These beliefs also imply that sex is all about the man's "needs" and pleasure, and procreation. There is no mention of pleasure for women being important. Intimacy is likely to be very unequal, and the submissive wife may never discover or express her own sexual preferences. The orgasm gap is often wide.

Sometimes, the man will use religious teaching to control the contraception (or lack of it) as well, meaning the woman has no control over her own body and pregnancies. In some groups, such as those seen in the Shiny Happy People documentary[36] in the USA, where they home-schooled their children with a curriculum from the Institute in Basic Life

---

[35] See the survey done by baremarriage.com) **https://baremarriage.com/2021/02/the-duty-sex-isnt-sexy-podcast/**

[36] *Shiny Happy People: Duggar Family Secrets* Prime Video June 2023

Principles which reflected these ideas also, such that they had no exposure to a mainstream scientific education, women are consenting to endless pregnancies without knowledge of the options or consequences for her health. This is not informed consent.

It is very difficult for women in these Christian communities to speak up if they are being raped or betrayed by their husbands. Their complaints will either be normalised – "you said yes at the wedding and that's all the consent he needs." Or minimised – "Surely your husband desiring you should make you feel good?" Or she, the victim, will be blamed – "You are obviously not giving him enough of it, you must pray harder for him and forgive. You need to submit." They feel trapped.

Married women who are experiencing sexual abuse feel used, objectified, and often like life is no longer worth living. They feel let down by God, as they kept their end of the bargain by being a virgin when they got married, and it is not the happily ever after that they were promised. They feel ashamed. They feel unloved. They have no one to talk to about it all, as they fear being blamed and shamed. They have been taught God hates divorce, so they are trapped and silenced.

This is not loving behaviour. These ideas are not grounded in love. They do not see men and women as equal human beings, and certainly not as people with divine worth. This kind of teaching is all about power, control and patriarchy. It totally ignores what a healthy relationship looks like, does not teach consent, and does not empower girls with the knowledge and self-esteem they need in order to make their own healthy choices regarding their bodies and relationships.

It seems to me that the conservative/fundamentalist/evangelical church has focused so much on morality, that basic human values, such as loving kindness, have been at best pushed to second place in importance, and at worst seen as unimportant.

I believe with all my heart that we need to start with loving kindness and use this lens as we think about morality, and especially the morality we demand from others. I would advocate that Christian marriage and relationships need to be distinct not because of virginity, heterosexuality and no divorce, but rather because each and every person in these relationships are highly valued, and because their wellbeing is prioritised. I think there is an urgent need to re-examine this moral code through the lens of love.

I sincerely doubt a God who is love is looking down at us and applauding when a couple are virgins on their wedding day. I suspect such a God would be delighted when they are concerned to establish each other's boundaries and respect consent in the relationship.

How can a God of love desire a couple to stay together when one is beating or controlling the other? Is God's reputation so fragile that it needs the institution of marriage to be more valued than the people trying to live it?

Needless to say, I am giving my own daughters the teaching that I received about sex and relationships. Instead of a highly prescriptive set of rules, and limited access to other information or viewpoints, I want them to have agency and autonomy over their own bodies, relationships and sexuality.

First, I am actually teaching them about what healthy relationships look like. We drop it into everyday conversation, when observing relationships on the TV, or in books we read together, or when they chat about their friendships and difficulties with their peers. We think about how a variety of people might be feeling in different circumstances and situations, and what might be healthy for them. They learn, through family life, how to respect one another, and share. They learn how to celebrate their own successes, and the successes of others. We all admit our mistakes and have the opportunity to learn from them without shame. We point out toxic behaviours and why they are harmful.

Also, we talk about consent. A lot. And this is done at school as well nowadays, where we live. From the 5-year-old learning to name her body parts, and that her body is her own, and that no-one else can look at it or touch it without her consent. To the older child understanding that "no means no" and that if her friend or sister does not want a hug, she may not force it on her. To tweens and teens exploring more explicitly what consent looks like in sexual relationships, and how to spot controlling behaviours. I am teaching them that they have a right to say "no" in any and every situation they wish to. They have language that includes "relationship red flags" and "toxic behaviours". We model age-appropriate consent in our home, and provide an environment in which they can develop the self-worth and self-confidence needed to be empowered to use their own voice.

We talk about porn, and what a pornified style of relating looks like, and what intimacy is. Pornography is now so widely available on the internet; we feel it is important our children know about it as soon as they have access to personal devices – or are exposed to friends with phones.

There is a growing body of evidence that pornography use is creating an increased sense of entitlement, amongst boys especially, to demand their sexual fantasies of their partner, without regard for her feelings or desires.[37] Pornography creates the opportunity for intensity, on demand gratification, without intimacy. It gives the consumer complete control and views the other person simply as a body, not a whole person, dehumanising and objectifying them. Pornography use is driven by a hunger and desire to consume.

Christian women have told me their stories of getting married, only to find their Christian husband was addicted to porn. When this was mixed with purity teaching beliefs such as that a woman must submit to her husband and keep him sexually satisfied, or it was her fault that he strayed, very damaging behaviours resulted. Some women felt obliged to act out his sexual fantasies, which were repugnant to them, and felt objectified and used. Others found their husbands had little interest in their wife's pleasure, and their sexual relationship was very one sided and completely controlled by the man.

Intimacy requires connection and emotions to be felt. Our young people need to know that their future partners should be treating them with honour, as whole people, and be ready and willing to listen to them and allow them to also discover their own likes, dislikes and desires in any sexual relationship. Such relationships should be based on equality and pleasurable for both.

We teach our children to identify emotions, allow them to be felt, and model regulating them. When children learn to suppress their emotions, they become out of touch with their true values and their ability to give or withhold consent.

---

[37] See for example BMJ 2022;378:o1975 British Medical Journal editorial on Young Women and Anal Sex

When they learn to listen to their emotions, they tune in to their true self, and learn to set the boundaries they need.

We build self-esteem and confidence, allowing them to discover their talents and weaknesses and value themselves as they are, and for who they are. We try to avoid name-calling, such as "you are lazy", and instead use language such as "when you did that, I felt this." We avoid blame and shame language, and instead try to point out when words or behaviours caused hurt or harm, with the goal of learning from this for the next time. Growth is celebrated, rather than perfection. All of this enables them to feel confident in all kinds of relationships with others.

Our tweens and teens choose their own style of clothing, and we never restrict this on the basis of what someone else might think of it. They are responsible for themselves, and not for anyone else. We do not teach them modesty teaching. We teach them their bodies are their own, and other people's reactions are their own responsibility. This is done within a context of respect, so that they also learn about respecting other people's customs and traditions, and not causing undue offence.

We encourage them to value their bodies, by the food they eat, through the physical activities they enjoy, and advising them to rest appropriately. We try to promote "being healthy' rather than any kind of body shaming language.

We make sure they know about contraception, and protecting themselves from STDs, so that they can make healthy, informed choices.

We talk about misogyny, sexual abuse and assault, equality and their right to protect and defend themselves. When Women's Aid workers visit their school and teach them about these things, we encourage them to reflect on what they learnt from the lessons, and discuss it further at home.

I am not teaching them that it is their job to make men control themselves. I am not teaching them that they should be virgins when they get married. I am not teaching them that sex is a commodity, or that their worth as human beings is tied up with their sexual activity.

I am not teaching them a set of rules and controlling their behaviour through shame. I am not coercing them to accept a set of values so that they will continue to belong and be accepted.

I want them to be informed, empowered girls, able to form healthy relationships, have wholesome conversations and make their own choices which will enable them to flourish and which are in line with their own values. I hope that they know they will always belong and be loved and accepted, no matter what those choices are. I am delighted when they act with loving kindness and respect for others and feel proud when they speak with love about themselves and others.

I hope they will experience mutually loving and intimate relationships. I sincerely hope that they will experience sexual intercourse as beautiful, and that it will happen when they are good and ready. I hope that sex will be just as enjoyable for them, as it is for their partner. I hope it will be fun! I hope that when they do not want it, or need to set a boundary, that they are perfectly comfortable declining, without any guilt or shame. I hope that they will know how to give and receive respect and love with their partners and that they will be equipped to express their sexuality in a healthy way, knowing how to protect themselves from unwanted infections and pregnancies. I hope that they will feel free and able to walk away from toxicity. I hope sexuality will be a part of their lives that contributes to their happiness.

*****

If you have been affected by purity culture teaching then I recommend the baremarriage.com blog and podcasts, and their book, "The Great Sex Rescue."[38]

---

[38] Sheila Wray Gregoire, Rebecca Lindenbach & Joanna Sawatsky *The Great Sex Rescue* Baker Books 2021

https://baremarriage.com/

Questions for reflection.

1. What moral code were you given regarding sexuality, when you were young?

2. What consequences did this have for you later in life?

3. How have your ideas and beliefs changed over time?

4. What do you teach your own children or young people in your life about relationships and sex?

You Must Be Silent

There is within me a part called Mr Silence. Ironically, he is loud and commanding. Perhaps you have one too? These are some of the things he might say.

"Children should be seen and not heard. Don't speak unless you are spoken to. You must be silent."

"Women should remain silent in church. They are not allowed to speak, but must be in submission. (1 Corinthians 14 v 34) You must be silent."

"Let a woman learn in silence and full submission. I permit no woman to teach or to have authority over a man; she is to keep silent. 1 Timothy 2v11-12. You must be silent."

"The husband is the head of the household and holds the God-given authority. His decisions will be honoured by God, even if they are not ideal. The wife and children must obey. You must be silent."

"It is dangerous to speak up, you will be rejected by your family and your community. You must be silent."

"It is dangerous to ask questions, they will realise you have doubts and are ignorant. You must be silent."

"Don't expose yourself by speaking. You must be perfect, and holy. If you speak, you will reveal your imperfections and lack of knowledge. You will be treated with contempt. Just listen and learn what they want to hear. You must be silent."

"Why are you feeling upset? He has every right to behave this way, it says so in the Bible. You are bad. You need to behave better, so he does not get angry with you. You are the problem. Everyone else manages to submit, and not cause problems. You must be good. You must be silent."

"Don't tell your teacher, pastor or anyone about this. You are just a young girl. They won't believe you. He is a pillar of the community, respected by one and all. And anyway, he does a lot of good for God, he saves souls from going to hell. You must not damage his Christian witness. You must be silent."

"Don't tell anyone about this. It's not really that bad. There are lots of good times. Focus on them. If you do speak, and anyone does believe you, you will lose your family. And then what would happen? It is too scary to think about. You must be silent."

"Shame on you for trying to tell that person about what happened the other night. What were you thinking? They were right to shut you down and tell you not to speak of such things, because it would ruin the witness of the church. You must be silent."

*****

Silencing. It is a powerful weapon in the hands of an abuser.

When a victim finally finds the courage to speak up, and report what happened to them years before, so often people question why they did not tell someone at the time. These questions are asked, implying that the person reporting is not telling the truth, or that they were too weak to speak up at the time. The question can even feel accusatory, that the victim, in maintaining silence for so long, has allowed other people to be exposed to the perpetrator's abuse and misrepresentation of themselves.

In fact, asking why someone did not speak up years ago, shows a lack of awareness of the power of the silencing messages women and children who are victims of abuse are indoctrinated with. It shows a lack of understanding of the power dynamics inherent in hierarchical relationships, churches and societies. It fails to examine the environment this occurred in, and what needs to change in order to make it easier for victims to name what has happened to them, and feel confident that if they speak up, they will be listened to, validated, supported and that there is a high chance that perpetrators will be stopped and no longer permitted to harm them.

Now, of course, not everyone who holds a hierarchical view of the Bible is an abuser. However, the power structure this creates is the perfect environment for abuse to develop, and silencing plays a large part in allowing this to continue to this day in some church families.

I began my own journey away from the patriarchal, complementarian understanding of Scripture when I read Craig Keener's book, Paul, Women and Wives[39]. In this book, he gives a thorough exploration of the key texts which are used to make women obey and stay silent, in their original context. He does a great job of showing how these verses were written at a time when women were not educated, so Paul is actually allowing women to learn for the first time. They do not preclude them then going on to be educators themselves, or mean they have to remain silent forever. They were the first step in giving women a voice.

Margaret Mowczko's website[40] is a rich resource for exploring the Biblical theology of Christian egalitarianism in depth, if you want to explore this further for yourself. I needed to study the theology of egalitarianism first, to free myself from the patriarchal rules I was conditioned with from birth, to then be able to give myself permission, as a woman,

---

[39] Craig Keener *Paul, Women and Wives* Baker Publishing Group 1992

[40] **https://margmowczko.com/**

to think for myself, and voice my own experiences and opinions.

As I did this studying, my understanding grew, that it is possible to interpret Scripture in different ways, without any lack of respect for the text or the Divine. I also understood that some people weaponize the Bible and use it for their own gain, harming others in the process. It took longer for this intellectual enlightenment to filter down from my head to my body and my emotions, and for me to feel truly empowered to speak from my own heart and experience. In fact, this is still an ongoing process.

The dawning realisation of the powerful silencing I had experienced as a child took a long time to understand, process and come to grips with.

In my childhood, controlling and abusive behaviour towards wives and children was legitimised by the supposed God-given authority of the man. Bible texts were, I now realise, taken out of context, read literally and weaponised. Women and girls were trapped by the teaching that they must submit to the male head of the household. We had no power or right to a different opinion or interpretation of Scripture. Teachings about people being sinners were twisted to erode self-esteem and self-worth, effectively eliminating any push-back. Women's roles and voice in church were tightly controlled by the men, and women who colluded.

As I deeply pondered the reasons why I never spoke up about abuse witnessed and experienced during my childhood at the time, I came to realise that there were several factors at play. I found I could have compassion on myself for my silence, and extend that to others who found themselves in similar situations. I offer you my thoughts in the hopes it will enable you to develop this understanding and compassion also, whether as a survivor yourself, or as someone who seeks to support survivors and create safer faith communities.

Children raised in these environments can react in different ways. Children's brains are still in development; the wiring pathways are being formed, they believe what they are told and their personalities develop, in part, in response to the environment that they are raised in.

First, children may just experience an abusive home-life as normal. They may have never experienced anything other, and may not visit other families much. Abusers can actively use normalisation techniques to raise their children thinking that what they are experiencing is "right" and "normal", and that any differences they may notice in other families are "not Christian" or are "strange".

If a child is experiencing emotional abuse from the parent, such as harsh punishments for stepping out of line, or contemptuous comments if they ask a genuine question, or withdrawal of approval/attention/affection if they make a mistake, the child may withdraw and become silenced. If venturing a different opinion, having a question, or risking making a mistake feels too dangerous, then it is safer to hide, not say much, and toe the line. They may become people-pleasers from a very young age, always doing what the adults around them want, and never developing their own sense of self, likes, dislikes or opinions.

It is very unlikely a child will volunteer to disclose emotional abuse, or controlling behaviour in the home, because they think it is normal, they want to please their parents to gain some approval, and if they realise there is a problem at all, they think they are the problem. Children internalise blame. It is too dangerous for a child to imagine the care-giver is at fault, because they need the adult in order to survive. If they blame themselves, it gives them some sense of control and ability to keep themselves safe, albeit by hiding and keeping silent.

Other children will develop the same aggressive, manipulative, gas-lighting and controlling behaviours they see modelled by the perpetrator.

Children witnessing and experiencing coercive control, see one parent with the power and control, and the other parent colluding and enabling. They do not see anyone standing up to the abuser. The church can also too often appear to be enabling the abuse. Teachings such as "God hates divorce", "You must forgive 70 times 7", "You need to pray more", can all be used to collude with the abuser. What the women and children need to hear and see modelled is "God liberates the oppressed and hates abuse", and "You have immense value."

And then, there is the scandal of the cover-up. How many times have victims courageously tried to speak up, only to be shut down by the message that they should keep quiet to not damage the Christian witness of the individual or the Church? Far too many is the answer. Let's be very clear. Christian witness (or reputation) is not damaged by people speaking up about abuse. It is destroyed by the perpetrators every time they choose to abuse someone, and by those who know about it and choose to stay silent, or counsel women and children that they should forgive, and stay in abusive relationships. It is hard for victims to realise this, until they are freed.

Patriarchal cultures are not just found in churches. I lived in a Latin American village for 13 years, where the culture was machismo, and men held much of the power because they were the bread-winners, and the woman lacked education and income. Many of these families attended either the Catholic church, run by the male priest, or patriarchal evangelical churches. As their doctor, I heard countless women and girls telling me of physical, verbal, emotional and sexual abuse that they felt powerless to escape from. People again sometimes did not realise what they were describing was abuse and assault, as it was the cultural norm. They most often did not report crimes for the same kind of reasons as I described above. Some did not speak up because it would bring shame on family members. For others it was because it was a local church leader perpetrating the crime and paying for the child's education in exchange. Others hid the abuse because it would have led to a worse beating later on. It was a culture where 12- and 13-year-old girls were called promiscuous when they were found to be pregnant, and were made to live as the wife of the adult father of the child, who was actually their rapist, but never named as such.

With a few notable exceptions, the church there too was silent regarding gender-based violence. Indeed, its conservative, patriarchal teachings reinforced the power of the perpetrators in the main.

When I returned to the UK, I found some churches doing things differently, with good attention to safeguarding, members who notice abusive behaviours, listen to victims, report disclosures appropriately and support survivors. I found some Christian charities working hard to educate and inform the church about safeguarding issues and domestic abuse, such as Restored[41] and ThirtyOneEight[42].

However, I also found Christians continuing to weaponize Scripture, trying to silence and cover up abuse. As I started to speak about my own experiences, I found other women

---

[41] **https://www.restored-uk.org/**

[42] **https://thirtyoneeight.org/**

struggling spiritually, emotionally and psychologically as a result of growing up in similar churches.

Some of these women had not experienced controlling or abusive personal relationships, but had experienced harm from not being permitted to lead services, preach or be part of the leadership team of a church. They told how being restricted in using their voice, purely on the basis of their gender, left them feeling less than, and unloved by God. They made themselves smaller, did not speak up, even when they were more knowledgeable or experienced than the man, and felt inferior. They described that to be female felt synonymous with faulty or damaged goods. Some fought for the right to preach or be included in the eldership of the church, only to receive put downs from the men such as being told, "Women are too emotional to lead. They cannot be trusted spiritually." This resulted in some women feeling traumatised by the relentless put downs. They felt more loved, valued and respected by men they met outside the church, than within.

It is possible for women to start a journey to finding their voice. Women who grew up in a healthy home, and later found themselves in an abusive relationship, describe losing themselves and their voice in the face of endless coercion, threats, manipulation and gaslighting. Children who grow up in an abusive home, or in the grip of high-control religion, never form their true self in the first place.

My journey began as I started to discover my true self.

True self is called Immortal Diamond, by Richard Rohr[43], the Self in psychotherapy such as Internal Family Systems[44],

---

[43] Richard Rohr *Immortal Diamond* SPCK 2013

[44] Richard Schwartz *No Bad Parts* Vermilion 2023

Beloved by Henri Nouwen[45], Gabor Mate[46] calls it Authenticity. These authors became my teachers, as I realised that I needed to start getting in touch with, and listening to my own inner voice, in order to start living from a place of wholeness and truth.

I started listening to Lectio Divina[47], lying in the dark, evening after evening, while waiting for my toddler to drift off to sleep, and heard over and over again that I am Beloved.

Something in me fundamentally shifted, when I stopped believing "I am a worthless sinner," and started believing "I am beloved", "I am an equal, precious, human being with intrinsic worth," "I am a treasure." My tense body started to relax, and breathe more deeply.

It did not make me selfish or big-headed.

It made me able to see more of my own shadow; my own fears, weaknesses, self-hatred and damaging behaviours. The more I valued myself just for who I intrinsically am, the less I needed to defend myself, hide, or cover-up my mistakes. The more I became aware of my light and my shadow, the more compassion I had for myself, and the more I could see the parts of me that needed to step back and take a rest, like Mr Silence.

It is an ongoing journey. The more compassion I have for myself, warts and all, the more I can interact with others with

---

[45] Henri Nouwen *Life of the Beloved* Crossroad Publishing 2002

[46] Gabor Maté *When the Body Says No: The Cost of Hidden Stress* Vermilion 2019

[47] I was introduced to this Spiritual practice by Sharon Garlough Brown in her book *Sensible Shoes* IVP 2013. She offers free daily Lectio Divina on her website **http://www.abidingway.life/**

compassion. I see them as fellow human beings, with infinite value, wounds that need to heal, wonderful gifts to share and their own journey to travel.

Discovering my value enabled me to deconstruct the beliefs that were erroneous, damaging, silencing and belittling me. I started to trust my inner voice: my intuition. I started to notice when I was saying "yes", when I wanted to say "no", and gave myself permission to respond authentically. I started to value my body, and to listen to it. I found it is true that "The body does not lie". I started to listen when my body felt tense, anxious or defensive, and put appropriate boundaries in place to care for myself and recognise my limits.

Allowing my sense of self-worth to become embodied meant I could grieve the past. How I grieved the lack of unconditional love, that each child should experience from birth. And I could feel again. Feel the anger, rage and storm, and the sadness. I wept. And I was comforted.

And I knew none of it had been my fault.

I then had the courage to verbalise my true values, beliefs and ideas. I am learning to be curious, and develop clarity. I can think creatively about today and tomorrow. The world feels full of possibilities and adventures. I can live more of my day from that true self centre, feeling calm, confident, able to connect with others and show compassion.[48]

Living a life in which I am allowing my true self to emerge from the chrysalis feels like peace, joy, hope and love. It feels like freedom. It feels like I am embarking on the life I was born to live. It feels like coming home.

---

[48] The 8 Cs from Internal Family Systems therapy – Richard Schwartz

And I have now found my voice, and talk back to Mr Silence.

"Thank you for the years when you silenced me to protect me and keep me safe. I am no longer in those circumstances. I have worked hard to make sure my current relationships and friendships are respectful. I will never again be part of a church with a patriarchal leadership structure, because I do not find that a safe place to be. I now choose to listen to the oppressed, to the wounded and seek to offer them a safe place to tell their stories and be heard. I now choose to speak, and use my voice, to ask my questions and offer my opinions. I choose to speak up for the voiceless, to break the silence, and say #metoo, #churchtoo. And I hope to be able to use my words to set others free."

Discovering your worth, listening to, and letting loose your true self, living authentically, and speaking your truth enable you to take up the space that is yours in the world. It enriches each and every one of us. We all need to be challenged and stretched by each other's questions. We grow and expand as we experiment and explore. Our families, communities and societies need women and men who are able to show up, be vulnerable, have courage, and share their wisdom and experience and offer a different lens on issues, if we are to grow together in love, freedom, compassion and truth.

I hope this book is helping you glimpse a different path, giving you permission to unleash your true curiosity, and guiding you on the journey of transformation. We do not want you to be silent. We want to hear what makes your heart sing.

Questions for reflection.

Q1. How have you been silenced?

Q2. How would you describe your voice now?

Q3. What are the barriers to you speaking your truth?

Q4. Try noticing today, or this week, when you say "yes" when you want to say "no" and vice versa. Make a list. Then think, why did you not give your authentic answer?

Q5. Where could you use your voice to make a more authentic contribution this week?

Divorce and estrangement

Divorce

"Remember, marriage is for life!" an older woman at my wedding sternly told me. It sounded like a threat. At the end of that long day, spent celebrating with the extensive extended family of my husband, we returned to our little house, to find a friend had been in to decorate our bed with a banner that had our names and the declaration "for 50 years or more." It was meant as a congratulation, but felt like pressure.

To divorce was to fail in my religious upbringing. I think the only reason divorce was allowed was adultery, and even then, if the spouse repented, you were expected to forgive. A divorced person remarrying was frowned upon. This remarriage was considered adultery. You could only remarry if your previous partner had died. In Britain, we saw this played out in the Royal family, as King Edward VIII, as head of the Church of England, was made to abdicate the throne in order to marry a divorcee. Society's attitudes changed over the coming decades, with Charles, a divorcee himself being allowed to remarry a divorcee and still become king. As attitudes in society relaxed, some churches became more insistent on strict rules regarding divorce as evidence of holiness and being set apart. In these circles, "Christian marriage" became more and more venerated and protected at all costs, as it was seen as a witness to the world of God's standards.

Other teachings added to the feeling of shame that divorce created. The injured party was expected to forgive endlessly. Women were expected to submit and obey, deny themselves and sacrifice. A woman standing up for herself was an expression of pride. The victims of abusive behaviour were told "All sin is sin, there is no sin that is worse than another, hence deserving of a divorce." They were expected to stay and pray for their partner – or perhaps leave and pray for their partner's repentance and reconciliation. Divorce and moving on was not an option. People were encouraged to pray for a miracle, to expect the God who can do anything to move hard hearts and renew the marriage. To give up on this was to lose faith, to lack trust in the omnipotence of God. It was to doubt God and disobey.

Many a time, when asked why they stayed, I have heard an abused woman say, "I took my vows seriously. I promised to death do us part, and meant it." Being faithful and true is highly valued in the Christian church, and especially in high-control denominations. Such people can be depended upon. You know where you are with them. They are also vulnerable to putting up with and allowing toxic behaviour to continue a lot longer than is healthy for them. They can be controlled. When being loyal is so highly valued, there is also shame in finally ending the relationship. Again, it feels like a failure. The consequences can feel too messy and huge to face. There can be a real fear that admitting defeat, and filing for divorce is also asking to be condemned to hell for all eternity.

As we have seen in purity culture, women were taught that she should give her husband more sex if he strayed, and that if she satisfied him, he would not do it again. Women were taught to pray for their husbands more and more fervently if his behaviour was upsetting, and that her prayers could change him. Women were taught a version of the prosperity gospel regarding marriage – that if you pleased God, He would bless you with a happy marriage. It was a promise. The implication here was that when the marriage was not great, when prayers were not answered, when the infidelity was repeated, then it was the woman's own fault. She felt ashamed. She wished to hide what is really going on, because she feared she would be blamed and shamed for it.

There was also the terrible threat of dire consequences for the children should a couple divorce, in the teaching of the church. We were told that children would end up traumatised for life, should their parents divorce. Leaders claimed it was always better for the children if the couple stayed together as a family. Children of divorced parents were spoken of with pity, in hushed tones. If they displayed any behaviour problems, they were attributed to the divorce. Married couples gave the impression that they felt they were providing a superior upbringing for their own children; stable, safe and more Christian.

As a child, growing up with this teaching, any mention of divorce made me feel sick to my stomach. There was a deep fear of the stigma and other un-named dire consequences of such a thing coming to pass.

There was an attitude of "You made your bed, now lie in it," towards anyone who ventured to complain about their marriage. Perhaps it was easier to simply set a standard everyone was expected to reach "with God's help", than engage in the dirty, painful business of hearing terrible suffering and confronting harmful behaviour. There was pressure to show that "Christianity is good, because Christians don't divorce", and to present a good image to the world.

Gretchen Baskerville, in her well researched book, The Life-Saving Divorce, points out that while people say, "God wants loving marriages; Satan wants divorce," in reality, "God wants loving marriages, Satan wants cruel marriages."[49] It is not a necessary divorce that brings shame on the Church, it is abuse and infidelity that does that.

Justin and Lindsey Holcomb point out, "When a man chooses to be abusive, he breaks the covenant. An abusive man forfeits the right to remain married."[50] (The same would apply if it is the woman who is abusive.)

Trauma-informed research shows us that is the children who experience abuse and witness it happening to their parent, the children that grow up in a home where a parent is addicted to alcohol or drugs, the children with a narcissistic parent, who are very likely to experience long term mental, physical and psychological problems as a result. It is not the children who are saved from these situations by a life-saving divorce. Gretchen explains the evidence to back this up in her book.[51] Children who are in homes where there is abuse, repeated infidelity and conflict do better if the parents divorce, not worse.

So much of the teaching described above was effectively blaming the victim. If the victim prayed harder, was a better Christian, was a better wife or husband, then the spouse would behave better. All of that is simply untrue. No one can change someone else. No one is responsible for another adult's behaviour. People who believe these teachings will try harder and go on for longer in their marriages than

---

[49] Gretchen Baskerville *The Life-Saving Divorce Hope For People Leaving Destructive Relationships* Life Saving Press 2020 P102

[50] Justin Holcomb and Lindsay Holcomb *Does the Bible say Women Should Suffer Abuse and Violence?* JBC 28 no.2 2014

[51] Gretchen Baskerville *The Life-Saving Divorce Hope For People Leaving Destructive Relationships* Life Saving Press 2020 pp. 108-110

anyone else would consider reasonable. It is OK to say enough is enough and leave.

It is also important to remember that forgiveness does not mean automatically renewing a relationship. You can forgive someone and also leave that person to get out of the way of further harm. Submission and sacrifice are only healthy when it comes from a healthy sense of self. It is not good for anyone when it requires one person to be dehumanised. Everyone needs some boundaries to keep themselves safe. If these are violated, it is necessary and good to stand up for oneself. Some "sins" have graver consequences than others. Just because we all make mistakes does not mean we have to continue putting up with someone else mistreating us over and over again. It is healthy and good to set a limit.

Some claim that having compassion for the abuser, and the root causes of their abusive behaviour demands staying with them and never divorcing them. However, abuse is still abuse, and harmful to the victim, no matter what happened to the perpetrator in the past and contributed to them now choosing to act in an abusive manner. Never calling them out on their behaviour, refusing to shine the light, and not giving consequences for their actions, means that they are even less likely to ever face themselves, their own trauma, heal and change. Adults are responsible for their own behaviour. No one needs to constantly put themselves in harm's way, over and over again, when the other person shows no real evidence of change.

I have heard many stories of harm being done to people through these very restrictive views on divorce. Children have been traumatised through continuing to live in an abusive or high-conflict household, when divorce could have given them a more peaceful, loving, calm environment to grow up in. Victims of domestic abuse, sexual abuse, coercive control and betrayal trauma have stayed in these destructive relationships for decades, losing themselves and becoming ill, physically and mentally in the process.

It is high time for a rethink. Taking the lens of love to the human relationship of marriage, and more importantly to the people within it, is a good place to start. I now ask very different questions when someone tells me they are experiencing difficulties in their marriage. Are they safe? Can they live in accordance with their own values? What happens when they set boundaries? Are they respected? Are they able to give and receive loving kindness?

The church has the opportunity to teach on marriage and divorce very differently, with the well-being of the people involved at its heart, rather than a blind defence to the sanctity of the institution of marriage.

Teenagers can be taught about healthy relationships, red flags and toxic behaviours. They can be taught and shown their infinite value as beloved children of God, or simply as valuable human beings, who are worth being loved and respected. Marriage preparation courses can include exploring the themes of red flags, coercive control, consent and boundary setting and help people recognise early on if there are serious issues in the relationship. Marriage counselling can follow the example of secular relationship counselling, in not offering relationship counselling to people in marriages where there is abuse. The individuals need to be offered separate, private counselling in these cases to avoid colluding with manipulation and controlling behaviour. Sermons on divorce can talk about when separation is healthy, necessary and life-saving. They can talk about God's compassion and protection for the oppressed and victimised. Victims can be believed, validated and supported, without judgement or shaming. They can be empowered to make their own decisions about how best to protect themselves and their children, and to live a life where they can thrive.

Estrangement

Estrangement has a certain taboo attached to it. Adult children cutting contact with their parents, for example, is looked at askance even in secular society still, let alone in a religious context where forgiveness is highly valued, and sometimes weaponised.

We can understand why this might be. Historically, many cultures emphasized duty, obligations and responsibilities. People were very interdependent, and it was hard to cut yourself off from the support of your family. Elderly people relied on their children to provide for them in their old age. This is still the case today in many developing countries, where there is more poverty, less government benefits and a strong culture of the extended family being involved in every day living.

Western cultures nowadays promote independence. Adults are now much more self-sufficient, and do not need the financial and material support of the extended family in the way that they did in the past. People are empowered to set boundaries in relationships. They are much less likely to tolerate, for example, grandparents making comments that are in conflict with their own values, in front of their children. If such grandparents are unwilling to stop making, for example, racist comments in front of the children, the parents may decide this means an estrangement is necessary.

Despite this, the stigma remains. Health and social care professionals can still be heard commenting harshly about the children of an elderly person in a care centre, whose adult children never visit. Acquaintances of someone who has cut contact with a parent ask things like, "What do you tell people about that? Do many people know? Don't you feel guilty for not helping them when they are frail and infirm?"

The person who has initiated the estrangement, for very good reasons, can also feel guilt, shame and sorrow. They may experience pressure from other family members, or people in their religious community, to reconcile. This can cause an unhealthy cycle of reconciling and cutting contact for a period of time, until they realise that the other person is never going to change their behaviour.

Being raised in or part of a Christian church that teaches that forgiveness equates reconciliation, who see estrangement as "hating" the other person, and a lack of ability to forgive, can create a lot of internal and external pressure to conform and continue to engage with the perpetrator. There can also be pressure to keep reports of abuse within the church, and not go to the police, where restrictions on contact might be enforced by law.

Anyone considering going "no contact" with a relative, needs to be very clear in their own mind and heart of their own right and need to protect themselves from harm. They need to understand that forgiveness gives the choice of either renewing or releasing the relationship. It does not demand reconciliation. You can have no further contact with the person without harbouring bitterness and hate in your heart.

Estrangement can feel a huge decision to make, and is often only done after much deliberation and heart searching. And yet it is surprisingly common.

Karl Andrew Pillemer, professor of human development at Cornell University, US, carried out a nationwide survey for his 2020 book Fault Lines: Fractured Families and How to Mend Them.[52] The survey showed more than one in four Americans reported being estranged from another relative. British estrangement charity Stand Alone did similar research which suggests the phenomenon affects one in five families in the UK. [53]

Most often, adult children initiate the estrangement from their parents. However, it can also occur between siblings and other family members. The most common causes of estrangement are childhood abuse, antagonistic divorces, and conflicts in values especially regarding race, gender & sexuality and religious differences. People are also becoming more aware of how toxic relationships impact their own mental and emotional health. This can lead to a decision that estrangement is needed to protect their own mental health and allow healing.

Estrangement from family members can have some negative consequences. People may experience feelings of guilt. They may lose the support of family members. Children may not be able to enjoy the benefits of knowing their grandparents. There may be loneliness at times of family festivals such as Christmas. There is the absence of the stability that long-term relationships with people who have always known you brings.

However, usually people make this decision because the benefits outweigh the losses. Often, the family was already dysfunctional, and not providing the stability, care and kindness that a healthy extended family provides. The person becomes free from toxic, abusive behaviours. They

[52] Karl Pillemer Fault Lines: Fractured Families and How to Mend them Yellow Kite 2021

[53] https://www.standalone.org.uk/reports/ accessed 24.03.2025

experience peace and freedom. They can develop agency and determine their own friendships and futures. They can protect their own children from damaging verbal and other abuse. They can find the space and distance to heal.

Some Christians automatically judge estrangement as sinful. In reality, such decisions are taken in the context of very real suffering, and require much more nuanced understanding, compassion and support.

Sometimes reconciliation is possible. Some people are able to face their own behaviours and make changes. Sometimes therapy and/or mediation can facilitate the changes necessary for reconciliation to be a healthy choice.

But often, sadly, narcissistic, toxic people do not change. Sometimes the hurt and damage they have caused is so deep and serious, that renewing contact is simply asking for another wound to be inflicted. Educating ourselves on trauma and its physical, emotional and mental effects on people helps us to understand those who find this decision is necessary, and support them.

I cut contact with my father to stop the ongoing damage the relationship caused me, to give me the space and freedom I needed to seek healing, and to protect my daughters from being harmed. Later, bail conditions were set which made no contact legally binding. I feel sorrow. I have had to grieve losses these decisions brought. But I do not regret doing this. It was life-saving for me really. I feel relief, freedom and peace. My body is physically more relaxed and healthier.

In my work as a doctor, people tell me about their decisions to cut contact with relatives. I can listen to their story without judgement, and give them a safe space to express their emotions. There is always sadness involved, but there is often a process of healing going on also.

I also meet people who are plodding on in toxic relationships, wedded to the belief that it is their duty and responsibility, or trapped by enmeshment of some kind. Sometimes, there is betrayal blindness and denial still acting as their main survival mechanism. All too often, they are coming to the doctor because of the toll this is having on their physical, mental and emotional wellbeing.

When I encounter people on the other side of the story, whose relative no longer contacts them, I can listen to their stories as well. I can be part of the health and social care services that can provide them with the care and support they need, without judgement. As a society, we can provide care for the frail and infirm, when it is not appropriate or healthy for their own close relatives to do so.

Human relationships are complex. To anyone who is making or has made the decision to cut contact with a family member, I would just like to say, you are not alone. I believe you have done this for good reasons. I hope you find relief and freedom in your decision, and that it is part of a healing journey. Listen to your inner voice and act in accordance with your own values. Don't let others, looking in from the outside, place burdens and responsibilities on you that are not yours to carry. Little by little, day by day, make new connections that contribute to your mutual wellbeing. It takes courage to step up and do what is needed to protect yourself and others you are responsible for.

Be at peace.

Questions for reflection.

Q1. What were you taught about divorce when you were young?

Q2. How have your views on divorce changed as time has gone on?

Q3. What has your own personal experience of divorce been? How has that changed you?

Q4. What would you say to a friend in an abusive relationship?

Q5. What are your views on estrangement?

Q6. How have these changed over time, through the life-experience you have had so far?

Q7. How can you support someone who is estranged from a relative?

Who do you trust?

As is now my custom, this morning I sat cross-legged by the patio doors and gazed out at the beautiful, vibrant tulips currently gracing our balcony. It has a calming effect on my racing, anxious thoughts, and allows my new friend, Trust Yourself, to find space to sit peacefully beside me.

Trust Yourself has my grandpa's voice. When I was a child, he used to tell me the same story over and over again. "I felt so inadequate. I'd left school at just 14 years of age. I had so little education. I started work as a printer's boy, and then went into the army when World War 2 broke out. After the war, as a young adult, I had the chance to study to be a teacher. I could hardly believe it was possible. I remember I was in a University English Literature evening class. The postgraduate lecturer was explaining the meaning of the Windhover poem, by Gerald Manley Hopkins. He said the eagle buckled and fell. But I could see a different meaning. I thought the poet meant as the eagle soared, he buckled into his God-given purpose. In that moment, I knew I could trust myself. Listen to others, ask their advice, hear their opinions, but then always listen to yourself, and make your own mind up. Trust yourself."

Immediately I start to listen to myself, old friends jostle in, making a huge commotion. "Stop, stop, stop!" the preacher starts in commandingly. "You mustn't trust yourself. You are a fallen sinner. You don't know what's best for you, or your family. You must trust in Jesus, and His Word, the Bible. You must be humble, and submit to our teaching. The Bible is the infallible word of God. You cannot question it. Especially as you are a girl. Eve took the fruit you know. She was deceived by the serpent. Women are easily deceived and misled. They cannot correctly interpret the Holy Scriptures. That is why leadership is male. Women are emotional and weak. You must beware of your selfish desires. If you really have a question, you can ask the male head of your household to explain it to you. But really you just need to listen to Jesus and obey."

Gently, I turn back to Trust Yourself, and return to my contemplative sit. I listen to my body, and notice where the tension is today, and what it is saying to me. I gaze at the resplendent orange of the tulip in awe. And I believe my deepest, truest self is awesome too.

******

The Christianity I grew up in, taught me that believing and trusting in Jesus meant not believing in or trusting myself. The two were mutually exclusive. In fact, listening to and trusting myself was shameful. Asking questions was doubt, or a lack of faith. Another shameful thing. So, I believed in Jesus, with my whole heart. I really did. I read the books on apologetics and learnt the right answers to the "difficult" questions, without ever asking them. I read the missionary biographies and determined to follow in the footsteps of these giants of the faith. I believed humility meant serving others, without regard for yourself. So, I served in the church as a teenager, went on short mission trips in the holidays, and then went as a long-term missionary doctor. I trusted Jesus to keep me safe and provide for me financially.

To be clear, a lot of these activities were good things to do, and had positive outcomes. The problem was that, in the end, I was pouring from an empty cup, because self-care was non-existent. Worse – I was actively harming myself in some of the decisions I made. I was deliberately putting myself and my family in danger. I thought that providing for myself, caring for myself and protecting myself, was wrong, or showed a lack of faith. And, ultimately, I now realise, it was mostly driven by a desire to be accepted and loved. Because I thought it was wrong to accept and love myself.

Not trusting myself, meant an inability to set healthy boundaries for myself, and an inability to give authentic "yes" and "no" answers. I always said "yes" to anything that was asked of me. I did not say "no" when something was harmful for me, because I believed that suffering and sacrifice were part of a holy life. I believed I did not matter.

I was taught that women and girls were inherently unable to reliably interpret the Bible correctly. The serpent being able to deceive Eve was cited as proof that females are unable to discern good from evil. This was the reason given for spiritual leadership of the church being male – men were trustworthy and reliable interpreters of The Word.

I was told women were too emotional to lead a church. It was implied that showing emotion was a sign of weakness, and being easily swayed in one's opinion. Hard headed, logical thinking was what was needed to be a good church leader.

I was brought up in a faith that taught that the world, the flesh and the devil were evil. I believed that my body was evil, or at least, that its carnal desires would lead me astray, away from God and heaven, and that the physical was very unimportant compared to the spiritual and my soul. So, I paid very little attention to my body and appearance, and suppressed or ignored most aches and pains.

It took many years to come to the point where this worldview was no longer sustainable. I had to get to breaking point to start to peel away the layers and remove the glasses of denial. All my life, when I needed to make a decision, I had prayed "What do you want of me? Your will be done." It was a reflex. The moment I realised that I did not trust myself at all, but rather sought external direction for every new choice, was like a light coming on. Once I realised that I was in a high-control religion, that I was allowing to tell me what to do in very intimate details of my life, to my own detriment and its gain, I began to claim back my agency and learn to trust my own instincts.

Reading Bessel van der Kolk's groundbreaking book, The Body Keeps the Score[54], and Gabor Maté's When the Body Says No[55], introduced me to a new way of understanding my body. Both these books explore the now considerable evidence that our bodies do not lie. The traumas, suppressed emotions and decades of self-neglect inevitably become stored physically in our cells and organs, and result in diseases such as autoimmune disease (where the body attacks itself), addictions, skin conditions, bowel conditions, raised blood pressure, migraines, and reduction of telomeres that protect against harmful cancer genes being expressed. There is also an increased incidence of conditions such as irritable bowel syndrome, functional neurological disorder and fibromyalgia.

Once I laid aside the limiting belief that trusting myself was inherently wrong, I discovered that listening to my body was a healthy way to live my life, and an excellent way to learn to listen to my true self.

Emotions are so often expressed and felt physically. As I slowed down, and gave myself permission to feel, I began noticing all kinds of sensations and pains in my body that I had previously been unaware of. In turn, as I noticed the sensation, I began to ask what it was telling me, and then to be able to decide how I wanted to respond.

---

[54] Bessel van der Kolk *The Body Keeps the Score, Mind, Brain and Body in the Transformation of Trauma* Penguin 2015

[55] Gabor Maté *When The Body Says No: The Cost of Hidden Stress* Vermilion 2019

Our bodies are trying to communicate with us all the time. They are telling us when we are uncomfortable with something, and need to say no. They warn us of danger. They prompt us when we need to rest. They cry out when we are stressed and need to find solutions or create more margin in our lives. They niggle away when we are ignoring something we need to address.

The more we learn to listen to our bodies, the more we can learn to respond in healthy ways to the challenges we face every day. The more we learn to identify, name and articulate our emotions, the more they can guide us into appropriate action. When we face our traumas, and heal the wounds, symptoms of irritable bowel syndrome, migraine and functional symptoms can recede.

The religious upbringing I had also taught us that emotions are unreliable, and not to be listened to. We were taught that some emotions, such as anger, are wrong. Many proverbs were cited as evidence of the dangers of anger, and we were taught not to be angry at all.

All such teaching needs deconstructed, if we are to give ourselves permission to listen to ourselves and trust our own instincts. Anger, for example, is an emotion just like any other, not good or bad, it just is. When we feel angry, there is often an injustice happening. It can drive us to activism, to doing something to try to right the wrong. If we are not allowed to feel or express anger, we are vulnerable to being taken advantage of by abusive people. We may remain passive bystanders, when we should take action.

Anger is a necessary part of the process of forgiveness. I think it is impossible to forgive, and find peace, until you have felt the anger it caused you first. Underneath anger, there is often great sadness. There is something that needs to be grieved and released. If you feel the need to find this in the Bible, you will find it in the many Psalms of lament.

Suppressed anger comes out in other ways. It may be the person who flips into fight mode at the drop of a hat. Or the passive aggressive muttering, stomping and eye-rolling that is never expressed in clear, direct communication. Or it is found in the high blood pressure of the person who has never let go of an injury done to them.

Our minds, bodies and emotions are inextricably linked. Emotions cause the release of chemicals and hormones into the blood stream, such as cortisol and adrenaline. These cause our hearts to speed up, our blood pressure to rise, and can make us feel nausea. When we are stressed, our muscles contract and hold tension. As a doctor, I have found that the more a patient is open to listening to the emotions behind the pains, nausea and other symptoms that they come in with, the better the outcome. So often, the sore lower back is not just due to lifting something too heavy, but rather anxiety expressed in the tight, spasming muscles. If the patient is willing and able to look at the source of their anxiety, and address that, then the back pain takes care of itself.

The more we learn to listen to our bodies, and trust ourselves, the more we can learn to distinguish the symptoms of an emotional pain, and those that have a more organic cause.

People who experienced a home environment when they were children, where the adults did not regulate their emotions, or it was not safe for the children to express their emotions, may come to adulthood with a fear of emotional outbursts, or an inability to express much emotion. Dan Siegel explains this well in his Window of Tolerance model[56]. He explains that we want to be in the green zone, where we feel calm, relaxed and able to take on challenges. Stress and trauma can cause dysregulation and people become either hyper or hypo aroused. In the state of hyperarousal, they may feel anxious, angry or out of control. In the hypo-arousal state they may shut down, feel numb, exhausted and depressed.

Experiencing dysregulation can itself cause a fear of emotions. People fear they cannot trust themselves when in this state. But we can learn to expand our window of tolerance, through practicing activities such as listening to music, doing hobbies, and meditation. Such practices can be very useful tools in learning to listen to and trust ourselves.

We can change our view of our flesh. What if our bodies are miracles? What if they are to be enjoyed? What if they are an amazing gift that allow us to participate in the things we love most in life?

Now that I am a parent, I realise that should my children come to me and ask, "What do you want me to do with my life?" (as I did with God for many years), I would respond with, "I want you to live and enjoy your own life, and make your own decisions. I trust you and I want you to trust yourselves to make good choices."

What if that is what Divine love has been saying all along? What if the miracle of being human is the wonder of a life lived through flesh and bones, that are flecked with the divine? What if we were never meant to be controlled and coerced, but rather to live in freedom? What if living well means enjoying being who we are?

---

[56] **https://vimeo.com/377509039**   accessed 24.03.2025

More and more I find meaning and joy in learning to be present. When I am fully engaged, listening and responding, feeling and smelling, seeing and tasting mindfully, I discover that eternity is now. These moments can seem timeless. I feel calmer and more able to respond wholeheartedly, the more I recognise my true emotions and bodily sensations in the moment – the more I learn to listen to and trust myself.

The Japanese have a ceremony for returning soldiers. They are thanked for their service, and then asked to let that identity go, and return as a citizen, as something beyond a soldier. This is the journey I am on. I am letting go of the servant identity, of the doctor, missionary, or mother identity, and I am returning to myself. I am letting go of allowing other people, Jesus or the Bible to categorically tell me what I ought or ought not to do. I am returning as the person beyond those roles and responsibilities and rigid set of beliefs. I may (or may not) still fulfil some of the same roles, but they will no longer be my identity.

I now understand that humility does not mean blindly believing and serving other people. Humility is having a realistic sense of who I am, appreciating my strengths and aware of my weaknesses and being open to the strengths of others.

It has taken me a long time to come to the realisation that trusting myself is a good thing, a healthy way to live. But I can now tell you it is life-giving and soul-restoring. It enables me to feel my emotions and hear my needs and look after myself. It encourages me to be curious and open. It allows me to set some boundaries and show up whole-heartedly. It is an expression of faith that all life is sacred – including my own.

Questions for reflection.

1. Who were you taught to trust as a child?

2. How do you feel about trusting yourself? What emotions come up for you?

3. Do you easily express your emotions? Do you feel shame around any emotions?

4. Do you listen to your body? What practices help you do that?

5. How easy is it for you to stay regulated emotionally? Do you tend to get hyper or hypo aroused?

6. What practices do you or could you do regularly to help you become more regulated and aware of your emotions?

7. What is your next step towards trusting yourself more?

The Effect of Coercive Control and Narcissistic Parents on their Children

In chapter six we looked at the abuse of authority, narcissism in Christian leaders and some of the damage they can do. In this chapter I want to focus on recognising parental narcissism, emotional abuse and neglect, and how growing up in this kind of home environment affects the children. In particular, I will look at how this can play out in Christian families, where religion is used to further coerce and control.

Recognising Narcissism and High Control Religion

I first got my hands on a book about narcissistic parents[57] when I was already in my 40s. It was like a light bulb was switched on as I finally recognised what had happened to me as a child, and the profound effect it had on my development. So much of what I had assumed to be "normal" during my childhood was illuminated as emotional abuse and neglect, coercive control and spiritual abuse. Being able to name it as such opened the gate of my internal prison, and allowed me to start on the journey of deconstruction and healing. Once I saw it, I could not unsee it, and I began to recognise the patterns in all kinds of scenarios, and break free from my conditioned responses.

There are nine main traits of narcissism, according to DSM-5, (the diagnostic manual used by psychiatrists), which can be overt or covert.[58]

---

[57] Julie Hall *The Narcissist in your Life: Recognizing the Patterns and Learning to Break Free* Da Capo Lifelong Books 2020

[58] **https://www.psychologytoday.com/gb/conditions/narcissistic-personality-disorder** accessed 24.03.2025

1. Grandiosity. The person expects to be recognised as superior without grounds.
2. Fantasies of unlimited success, power or brilliance.
3. They believe they are special and unique.
4. They need excessive admiration.
5. They are entitled, believing they deserve special treatment, no matter the impact on others, and expect others to comply with their demands.
6. Exploitation. They use others for self-gain.
7. Impaired empathy. They do not recognise the feelings or needs of others. They use motivational empathy by guilt-tripping others for their own ends.
8. Envious of others
9. Arrogance and impaired self-awareness. They can modify their behaviour to avoid accountability, but do not change the behaviour that is harmful to others.

There is a spectrum of narcissistic behaviour, from what one might consider healthy assertiveness in the right context, through to full blown narcissistic personality disorder where the behaviours are toxic to others.[59]

First, I am going to consider how toxic narcissism plays out in parents. This parent presents themselves as intrinsically superior to others. The world revolves around them. They are the most important person around. They show contempt for others, including their children and belittle them. They expect others, including their children, to substantiate their status. Their needs are all important, and they ignore the needs of others, including the needs of their children. They feel entitled to money, time, sex, and see themselves as owning or possessing their children. They use others to meet their own needs, and do not care what the cost is to

---

[59] For a fuller description of narcissistic traits see Villiers & McKenna *You're Not The Problem* Yellow Kite 2024 Chapter 2

the victims, including their own children. They use fear, obligation and guilt to manipulate those in their control. They use motivational empathy to get what they want. They tell their children that if they don't do something the parent will feel sad, teaching the child to ignore their own feelings and not allowing a "no". They make the child responsible for the parent's feelings. To make sure the child prioritises the parent's feelings, they use the silent treatment – emotionally abandoning the child for days at a time. They never take responsibility for their actions or the effect it has on others. Their apologies consist of "I'm sorry if you feel that way", which is of course no apology at all.

The effect on the child is catastrophic. Instead of receiving nurture, being cherished and encouraged to flourish, they are used, belittled and exploited. They feel constant fear, obligation and guilt.[60] They are kept small, yet parentified and expected to manage the parent's emotions for them, and take on adult tasks before they are of an age to be capable of them. They are also expected to keep up the reputation of the adult. The fear of being abandoned by the parent and the sense of duty instilled in them from a young age keeps them compliant. They are not allowed to have any boundaries. They are treated as possessions, so they are dehumanised and objectified.

The other parent in this family is often an enabler. They are a victim themselves. And they may also fail to protect the children or leave. The child is helpless, dependent and has to adapt to survive. They witness the enabling parent walking on eggshells, doing all they can to keep the narcissist in a good mood, and see their fear and powerlessness. They may copy or scorn these behaviours.

---

[60] Described as FOG by Villiers & McKenna *You Are Not The Problem* Yellow Kite 2024 p154

They will also most often think this is all normal. Any negative feelings they have or harm done to them will be consistently minimised and dismissed.

Children in these families may well live in a clean house, with plenty of clothes and food to eat. They are often well provided for financially. They may well say they had a good childhood. They think love is transactional, that is it the child's duty to take care of the parent's emotions. They often deny or repress memories to create for themselves the illusion they were loved, because to admit the thought that this was not love, risks them discovering they are unlovable. "Whose own parents does not love them for goodness' sake?! Surely only children with something seriously wrong with them!" they think.

Roles in a narcissistic family

There are some typical roles that the children in these families fulfil. One child, often the oldest, or the oldest of the opposite gender to the narcissistic parent, will be a golden child. This child responds to the controlling, authoritative parenting by trying to be perfect. They develop perfectionist and people-pleasing behaviours and try to excel in the things the parent approves of. They do not feel safe expressing any opinions of their own, or breaking any rules. They may well be excellent students, very good, quiet children, who no one notices are totally unable to develop as their true selves. They are a projection of the parent. They have a constant anxiety inside them, and low self-worth driving their attempts to be good or to shine. A truly golden child will expect to continue on a pedestal into adulthood and may therefore develop narcissistic personality disorder themselves. A child who is enmeshed however, will be discarded by the parent if they start to develop their own voice and ability to say "no". They are no longer favoured by the parent once they see the abuse for what it is, or when they fail to continue to boost the image and reputation of the parent. This child emerges into adulthood with no sense of self, no idea what their own values are, or who they are as a person. They read the room and respond to keep everyone else happy. There are unaware of their own needs, let alone wants, and do not pay any attention to them.

Another child is often the scape-goat. They are blamed for everything and anything, deflecting any responsibility away from the parent. These children see the abuse much earlier on. They try to call it out and demand boundaries. They are never good enough, the butt of every joke and jibe, or totally ignored for months or years. Everything about them is rejected and they are silenced. These children often grow into adults with depression, anxiety, OCD, eating disorders, addictions, personality disorders, and have a lack of identity.

Where are there are several children, one may take on the role of the flying monkey. This child tries to keep themselves safe and in favour by taking the side of the parent perpetrating the abuse. The narcissistic parent plays the victim, and uses them to send their messages, and plead their cause. The flying monkey often tries to keep everybody happy by being the life and soul of the family, distracting themselves and everyone else from looking at the problems. They may develop narcissistic traits themselves, learning behaviours such as manipulation, gaslighting and smear campaigns to protect their illusion that the narcissistic parent is all they present themselves to be, and that the victims need to be kept quiet. They often scorn the enabling parent as weak.

The youngest children in a family may be invisible children. These children are overlooked and invisible to the rest of the family. They spend hours playing alone, are neglected and escape into fantasy worlds of books, TV programmes or daydreams. They become disconnected from their feelings and find it hard to form intimate deep relationships as adults. They too can develop mental health problems[61].

The impact of High Control Religion in these Families

High control religion being practised by the family can intensify the whole experience. The narcissist will claim God-given privilege (e.g. in patriarchal religion) and say things such as "children must obey their parents,", "women must submit to men" with divine authority that cannot be questioned. Alternatively, they may claim they are "called by God" to a particular "very important" spiritual role, and that this makes them more important than anyone else in the family. This will be used to justify their grandiosity and entitlement. As they are called by God, the children must serve their needs, as in doing so, they are serving God. The children must also protect their reputation, and keep silent when necessary, to protect the image of the church and God Himself.

The children will be taught that the whole family is special and superior to others, because they are being raised in the "truth" and "going to heaven", while their heathen neighbours and friends are not chosen, are sinful and destined for hell. This can create isolation for the children, either through making them wary of befriending children from non-Christian families, or outright forbidding it. The isolation limits their exposure to other points of view or experiences, and reduces the chances that they will notice that their own family is not a healthy one.

---

[61] Read more about this in Villiers & McKenna *You are Not the Problem* Yellow Kite 2024 chapter 7 and Julie Hall *The Narcissist in your Life: Recognizing the Patterns and Learning to Break Free* Da Capo Lifelong Books 2020 Chapter 8

Emotional abandonment and contempt will be justified by the adult telling the child they are a worthless sinner, who deserves punishment, the silent treatment or physical chastisement. The child will be told they were nothing more than a worm from birth, destroying their self-worth, and manipulating them to be grateful for the breadcrumbs of approval or affection that might come their way. This sets them up to be starving for love and affection in adulthood, and this is why they easily fall prey to partners who first love-bomb them, then abuse them, in the typical cycle of domestic abuse. They do not know what respect feels like.

The whole narrative of "Jesus died for your sins" can be used to guilt trip the children. They will be raised being told they should be grateful for their salvation, bought at such a high cost, so they must be good, quiet and obey. When they fail, they will be blamed and shamed, creating a cycle of fear, guilt and obligation, which will govern their behaviour and motivation. This may well continue into adulthood, making them adults who are easily manipulated and controlled.

Children will have the adult's expectations and projections put upon them. Instead of going to school to learn with curiosity and open minds, they will go feeling the obligation to evangelise their peers and tell them the "truth" that they have been raised in. Curiosity, I have come to realise, is such an important value to have in order to discover who you are, and to be able to form a wide variety of friendships and relationships. When a child is raised to be suspicious, closed, and always defending "the truth", their curiosity is shut down. This is a travesty of a childhood. Children are naturally curious. They spontaneously ask questions, experiment and discover. In this way they become themselves, and can interact with the world and other people in a healthy, open-hearted manner, accepting others for who they are, and learning from them. When this is shamed as "doubt" and framed as putting them in danger of hell, the result is children who grow into fearful adults. Whenever they encounter someone who is different, the reaction is more likely to be judgement and prejudice. It can take a lot of courage to break free from these beliefs and patterns.

God will be a toxic version of the divine in these families. God will be grandiose, superior, set apart and entitled to our worship and adoration. God will demand perfection, and reject, punish and not talk to anyone who fails and sins. The fear of hell will be ever present. The transactional "gift" of salvation and a ticket to heaven, will come with a heavy price tag. God will be perfect and pure, seeing us humans as dirty rags, worthy of contempt. Children will be expected to be always grateful and yet never good enough. Imagine for a moment living life like that – always telling yourself you should be grateful, while feeling a constant pressure to be perfect, and knowing you will never be good enough. It sounds more like a living hell to me, than a path to eternal joy and bliss.

Trauma Responses

Children raised in these environments will also develop trauma responses. This kind of adverse experience is prolonged, repeated and pervasive. It leads to complex trauma responses, categorised as Complex Post Traumatic Stress. Judith Herman's research found that trauma is not limited to one off catastrophes or wars. Rather it is our response to anything that feels overwhelming, anything that is too much, too soon, too fast and that threatens our sense of safety.[62]

---

[62] Judith Herman *Trauma and Recovery: from domestic abuse to political terror* Pandora 1992 p.33

Whether an event is experienced as traumatic also depends on protective factors. In the narcissistic family there may be other adults close to the child who show them unwavering positive regard and respect, and thereby mitigate some of the effects of the narcissistic parent. However, emotional abuse and neglect often produce very marked trauma responses in children.

There are 4 commonly recognised trauma responses.

- Fight

- Flight

- Freeze

- Fawn

Pete Walker describes these well in his book, Complex PTSD from surviving to thriving[63]. It is important to bear in mind a person may have more than one predominant trauma response that they are stuck in. The path to health is recognising these and widening the breath of responses to include all 4 at a proportionate level, when needed in the present.

Fight

People who are stuck in a fight response show some of the following characteristics; they will be narcissistic, explosive, controlling, entitled, type-A, perfectionist, sociopathic, or show a conduct disorder. They control to connect and rage to be safe. They are often perceived to be "difficult" or "demanding" people.

---

[63] Pete Walker *Complex PTSD: From Surviving to Thriving* Azure Coyote 2013 p12

Flight

People who are in flight-mode can be dissociative, panicked, rushed, worried, driven, adrenaline junkies, busy-aholics, micromanagers, perfectionists, have been diagnosed with mood disorder/bipolar disorder, ADHD, or have addictions. They perfect to connect and perfect to be safe.

Freeze

These people are co-dependent, contracting, hiding, isolating, a "couch potato", a hermit, a domestic violence victim, or have ADD. They are saying, "There is no way I will connect. I hide to be safe."

Fawn

People operating from this trauma response demonstrate servitude, obsequious attitudes, and a loss of self. They are the people-pleaser, the doormat, exhibit social perfectionism, and were the parentified child. They merge to connect and grovel to be safe. They often burn out through a lack of boundaries and an inability to say "no" to requests made of them.

Complex PTSD is found in people who have a history of trauma such as childhood abuse, domestic violence, an alcoholic parent, war, witnessing ongoing abuse, bullying etc. It is the experience of a thousand paper cuts, over a long period of time, often, although not always in childhood, which causes a trauma response. Certainly, many adults who were raised in families with a narcissistic parent, and those exposed to spiritual abuse as a child develop cPTSD.

These people experience some of the same symptoms as people who experience PTSD following a single trauma. These are flashbacks, avoidance, and either hypervigilance or numbing. The flashbacks in cPTSD are more likely to be emotional, than visual. This is when people are triggered to feel emotions from past trauma by current innocuous stimuli. They can shut down and dissociate or go into panic mode for days sometimes.[64] I think, for example, of the patient who described panic attacks happening when their partner initiated sexual contact. They had a history of sexual abuse. Or the patient who described being on a walk with their family, and fearing they were lost. Their ears hummed, they felt dizzy and sick, they could not speak or engage with their partner until they were back to the car park. In their childhood they had experienced being taken on dangerous walks by their narcissistic parent, and being jeered at for crying with fear. This was in the context of other abuse. These are emotional flashbacks.

In addition, to be diagnosed, people also need to have the following 3 symptoms;

- Negative self-concept (low self-worth)

- Difficulty with emotional regulation (small green zone of tolerance)

- Difficulty with relationships (connection and trust is disrupted)

Instead of emerging into adulthood with a healthy sense of self, an ability to set boundaries and expect respectful behaviour, self-confidence and an innate sense of direction, children who survive emotionally and spiritually abusive childhoods emerge with complex trauma. The horror of this is that it effectively means they have no idea who they are or what their own values are. They are ignorant of what a healthy relationship looks like and either scared of intimacy

---

[64] Pete Walker *Complex PTSD: From Surviving to Thriving* Azure Coyote 2013 p3

or become co-dependent and easily fall prey to abusers in adulthood. Their own behaviours can be erratic, harmful, or evasive, making it hard for them to make friends. The damage done can be immense and have lifelong implications.[65]

And yet there is hope. First of all, my hope in writing this book is to help survivors understand what happened to them, and most of all that it was not their fault, they are not to blame. I also hope that it will raise awareness and educate folk to be more able to spot harmful beliefs and behaviours and have the courage to call them out and speak up for the vulnerable.

Second, there are paths to healing. You do not have to remain stuck. It is possible to deconstruct, grieve the losses and terrible injustices, understand it was never your fault that this happened to you, and see a light in the distance that is beckoning you towards love, freedom and peace.

Paths to Healing

The paths to healing are as varied as there are people embarking on them. They are not linear. They take many twists and turns, and sometimes go back on themselves. They require different tools at different junctures. It can feel like peeling an onion, there are so many layers to it.

When I first came out of denial and started on this journey, I felt frustrated that I could not find a four-point plan that told me the stages I needed to go through in order to get to my destination (which I could not define either).

Now, I define my goal as moving towards engaging with the world with the qualities listed in Internal Family Systems

---

[65] Laura Anderson *When Religion Hurts You* Brazos Press 2023 p35

therapy (developed by Richard Schwartz), which are compassion, creativity, curiosity, confidence, courage, calm, connectedness, and clarity[66]. My goal is to be living each day with authenticity, being true to myself, able to set boundaries, and respect those of other people.

The route to getting going on this lifelong journey certainly involves deconstruction. It requires developing self-awareness, so that we notice when we are acting out of certain core beliefs and start to question their validity.

Some people can do this gradually. I found I came to a point where I literally felt like I was sitting on the floor each morning, emptying more and more beliefs out of my head on to the floor around me, and examining each one thoroughly. After a period of some months, I started to very carefully choose which ones I put back in, or wished to redefine, and which ones were to be swept up and discarded.

Practically speaking, this process needed time alone, time to read/listen to podcasts, time to meditate, and chats with trusted friends.

Becoming aware of what really happened in the past and the work of deconstruction provokes grief. Grief includes sorrow, anger and acceptance. It requires expression and processing of emotions. These are felt in the body, shouted to the hills, thrown into the sea, and scribbled in a journal. Sometimes they are sobbed out in a bear hug. Sometimes they are painted out with a therapist, or punched into a pillow. There are those that can be expressed to a loved one. And others that need the safety of a professional.

---

[66] Richard Schwartz *No Bad Parts* Sounds True 2021 p98

Certainly counselling, psychotherapy or EMDR treatments can be an important part of the journey, and different kinds of therapy can be needed at different times.

There is a need to reconstruct also. We need to get in touch with our own current values, and learn to live and speak in line with them. Instead of living how we have been told we must, we now need the courage to listen within, trust ourselves, notice what our bodies are telling us, and give our true opinions and responses. At first this can feel terrifying and cause guilty feelings. It takes courage to persevere. But the rewards are a peaceful mind and a rested body. It also leads to true connection.

Ultimately, it is a journey, not only towards our own selves, but also towards other people. For so long, we have lived a lie really. Never showing our true self, scared of being rejected as not good enough, or unlovable again. The amazing reward for those who are able to follow this path, is finding deeper connection, love and friendship is possible. The real you is very lovable and wonderful too. You can keep yourself safe in the world, while surrounded by people, and in the wild places too. You start to notice small ordinary everyday moments as awesome, and can stop to enjoy them and breathe.

It is also true that there are some who are unable to go on this journey with you. Some will stay stuck as the enabler or the flying monkey. That hurts. The boundaries that you need to keep in place cause sorrow. And are necessary. You will need to let go of the hope that the narcissist will change. You can only change yourself. And that is worth doing.

Others will stay stuck in the unhealthy religious community you have left, or are now on the fringes of. Maybe you can be a voice there. Maybe you choose to use your voice elsewhere. The important thing is that you can now recognise healthy spirituality and make your own choices, be free from fear and should and ought, and live freely.

Take your time. There is no rush. It is all about the journey.

Questions for reflection
1. Have you encountered narcissism? When, where, what happened?

2. What are some of the core beliefs and trauma responses you developed as a result of your childhood (if applicable)

3. If you come from a narcissistic family, which role(s) did you play?

4. If you experienced high control religion, what effects did it have on you?

5.What are your current values? What three values are most important to you?

6. How healthy are your current close relationships? What areas do you struggle with?

7. How are you getting on learning to express and process your emotions?

8. What would living life wholeheartedly look like for you?

Healthy Spirituality.

"Dare to believe. And when believing lets you down,

and after you have grieved, believe in something bigger.

Keep going until all that you have faith in is the earth, life, and everything.

Love. And when love lets you down,

and after you have grieved, take your love further.

Keep expanding the circle until all that you love is the earth life, and everything."

Gideon Heugh[67]

The focus of this book has been examining damaging, unhealthy beliefs and resulting behaviours, in order to create space for something new. When the rules we were given as children were presented as absolutes, black and white, all or nothing, it creates a fear of daring to question or, heaven forbid, rejecting them. It takes courage – and often coming to a place of suffering – to be willing to take a second look, start to get curious, and acknowledge the doubts and questions that have always existed within ourselves.

It is risky to break the mould, and be authentic. We risk rejection, no longer belonging and a loss of community. We

[67] **https://gideonheugh.com/2023/04/14/reflection-life-is-so-much-audacity/** accessed 25.03.2025

may be called the black sheep, prodigal or fallen. It is necessary to count the cost.

But, unhealthy, high control religion and spirituality leaves people feeling divided, anxious, fearful and coerced. It is created from absolutes, objectification, censorship, obligation and exclusion. It controls. It makes the victims repress their emotions and it violates their boundaries. There is no room for debate outside of certain prescribed topics. The victims feel trapped. They feel a lack of self-worth and that they are never good enough. They feel manipulated and controlled.

The positives of belonging, feeling you are right, and knowing the formula for success can keep you going for quite a long time. But in the end, that voice within that is protesting will find a way to be heard, and the lack of inner peace will start to fragment you.

Healthy spirituality feels like an invitation. As soon as spiritual leaders and directors start to use the words "you are invited to..." it feels safer. People are permitted to choose. Life, soul, spirit feels spacious and free. It leads to liberation, expansion and curiosity. There are no forbidden questions, musings or experiences. Suspicion and judgement are suspended. The heart feels open, and the mind free to enquire. Individuals and communities are at liberty to make their own choices. Morality is not a purity code, but rather guided by loving kindness. There is a sense of peace and wholeheartedness. Healthy spirituality thrives on awe and wonder, and embraces mystery. It feels abundant, loves diversity, and is inclusive of all.

Most of all, I am discovering, healthy spirituality is a path to transformation.

For me, healthy spirituality feels more like poetry than an instruction manual. The religion I grew up in was the ten commandments, transaction, punishment and shame. It was a formula for getting to heaven. It was narrow, restrictive and tunnel vision. I have discovered a love for poetry because it invites, is curious, it ponders, it embraces mystery, and expresses beauty and love. It does not seek to provide answers, but rather invites the reader to ask new questions. It shines light from different perspectives to illuminate facets we never imagined existed. It expands our awareness. It slows us down. It invites us to savour, muse and relish. Poetry can inspire gratitude, express deep emotion and open us to transformation.

Ken Wilber described personal development in terms of four dimensions; growing up, cleaning up, waking up and showing up. It is another way of describing this path of transformation. Richard Rohr comments that traditionally the church mainly focused on cleaning up, and did that poorly, focusing on purity codes, rather than transformation of consciousness.[68]

Growing up describes the process of maturing emotionally and psychologically that most people undergo throughout the course of their life. This is the child who moves from melt downs and tantrums to becoming emotionally regulated and able to recognise and express their own needs. It is influenced by the culture and microcultures within which the person lives. Exposure to difference – through moving out of home, travel, getting to know people from different backgrounds – gives the opportunity to develop greater insights, tolerance and compassion. Love and suffering, as people become parents, lose loved ones, and experience

---

[68]   **https://cac.org/daily-meditations/growing-up-waking-up-and-cleaning-up/**   accessed 25.03.2025

trauma of different kinds, can be the catalyst to developing depths of empathy.

Cleaning up requires self-awareness. It is the process of acknowledging your shadow self – those parts of yourself that you do not like or try to hide – and integrating them all. Becoming aware of them in itself goes a long way towards disarming the defences we have created to hide and protect them. It helps create limits on our ego and false self that we project in the world. It enables us to do the work of getting to know our true self, and having the confidence to be ourselves. It gives us a sense of humility, knowing we are just as human as the next person, with all our weaknesses and strengths, so we are able to behave in more compassionate ways with our fellow human beings.

Waking up are the spiritual practices that we find help us move towards union. It is the journey from seeing ourselves as separate to that of feeling ourselves as intricately connected with nature, animals and other people. It is the practice of loving kindness towards all living things. It moves our focus from the personal and independence, to living as interconnected communities.

Showing up is the result of the other stages. The more we know ourselves, warts and all, and accept ourselves, the more we will be able to engage as ourselves with those around us. We lose the defences we create to protect fragile egos and wounds as they are exposed and heal. We discover the person we truly are and are able to make our contribution to the world. We show our concern for the suffering of the world, and engage in playing our part in creating loving, peaceful, accepting communities where people can feel loved and safe.

Healthy spirituality does not require someone else's values to be imposed upon you. It means being free to be true to your own values. These values can also change priority and evolve throughout your life. What is most important to you as a young adult with few responsibilities may be different to your values as a parent, and your values when infirm.

If you have come out of high control religion, and especially if you grew up in a spiritually and emotionally abusive home, then you are likely to need to examine the values that you were given, redefine them, and then choose the ones that resonate most with you in the present moment.

Let me give you an example. Google a "list of core values". First, go through the list fairly speedily, sorting the values into three columns.

Very Important	Somewhat important	Not important

Here is an example of how your table might look

Very Important	Somewhat important	Not important
Authenticity	Making a difference	Self-expression
Kindness	Fun	Efficiency
Inclusion	Knowledge	Patriotism

Usually lists of values have 50 or more, so your actual table will be bigger, but let's use this as an example.

The next step is to think about how you define these values, has this changed over time, and why you put them in those columns.

For example, this person might say that in the past authenticity was not on their radar. They believed they had to be what Jesus wanted them to be, not their true self, because this was evil. Putting this as very important is a reflection of now understanding the path to peace and showing up in the world requires authenticity. It has become very important to them.

They might say that in the past making a difference was very important to them. They lived their life for others, trying to win esteem and approval this way. This led to burn-out. Now, they still want to be kind and helpful, but not at the expense of themselves. So, it is somewhat important.

They say putting self-expression in the not important column was a reflex reaction. It was so condemned in their childhood that it still feels terribly wrong to them. On reflection, they would like to move this value to being somewhat important, as it is something they would like to learn.

Efficiency is not important to them because this was weaponised against them as a child and they were repeatedly shamed for being slow and inefficient. They now believe love is not efficient and do not value this.

In contrast, fun was forbidden in childhood. It was not valued at all, and the ways they could keep themselves safe involved being responsible and doing the jobs well. So, it is now something that they wish to include in life and learn.

Knowledge has kept them safe in life, and enabled them to develop their career. They love to learn and study and apply it to many aspects of their life. Patriotism is not important to them, because they have lived in different countries, have friends and family from different cultures, and they value diversity and inclusion of all, not belonging to a particular group.

Kindness is the ultimate expression of love for them. When someone is kind to them, they well with tears, it is so appreciated. They very much want to always try and be kind to others and make them feel loved.

Inclusion is important to them, as they were only included in their religious group of origin while they conformed. Now, their thinking and their heart have expanded with a deep desire to make everyone welcome. They know how it feels to be rejected when you express who you really are.

Your own list and columns will be unique. Your reasons for choosing your most important values will be your own. There are no right or wrong answers. It is about getting to know yourself, as you are in this present moment, and is a chance to further reflect on how you are growing and transforming.

Being conscious of your current values helps develop that sense of self. It also enables you to intentionally live each day in line with those values, and spot the times when you are not true to yourself.

Another exercise which is useful for this path of transformation and growing in your authenticity, is to pause at the end of each day. In the pause ask yourself a couple of questions.

Did I say "Yes" today when I wanted to say "No"? When? Why? How will I do it differently next time?

Did I censure my speech today? Did I fail to say something I wanted to? Or agree with something that in truth I disagree with? Why? How can I do it differently tomorrow?

When did I show up as myself today? How did it feel? How did t help me connect with others/nature or feel part of something bigger than myself?

Deconstruction is a process of examining the beliefs you were given or adopted, to decide if you still believe them and if they line up with your own values and higher power. The process is often triggered by discovering the harm that has come from those beliefs. It is hard work, and carries risks. The more firmly you held those beliefs and followed them with all your heart, the greater the hurt and disillusionment encountered, once the cognitive dissonance becomes too hard to bear. But it often does become too hard to bear, and the process of deconstruction clears the rubble and makes way for something new to be built, or a different kind of clarity of purpose and connection with others in the second part of your life.

People end up in different places after deconstructing. Some leave more fundamentalist churches and migrate to more liberal, ecumenical congregations. Others would still call themselves Christian, but no longer attend a church. Some hold on to a belief in God, but would no longer say they are part of any religion in particular. Others become agnostic or atheist. There are also those who, as Mike Petro on the Everything Belongs podcast[69] put it, are both God-believing and atheist.

Wherever you find yourself, (and this may change again in future!), I think it is important to be able to recognise what a healthy spirituality and spiritual community looks like.

I would say that it needs to be rooted in love, but I hesitate to use the word love without qualification, because it was so misused in my experience. What we were told was "unconditional love" was in fact totally conditional on accepting certain beliefs to be included. We were told it was all "grace" and then made to feel we needed to spend the

[69] Everything Belongs, a podcast from the CAC

rest of our lives earning it. Any love we were shown was only breadcrumbs.

So, I prefer to use words such as Kind, Diverse, Inclusive and Open. It is a spirituality that casts out fear. It is patient, honours others and is not easily angered. It is a spirituality that creates trust and hope. It accepts, and encourages one another. It is not afraid to expose hurtful actions and will make sure it is safe for people to be vulnerable. It guides along the path of transformation and union.

Difference is celebrated and embraced.

It is a space where you enjoy being you, and can show up and play your part.

Questions for reflection.

1. How has your spirituality been unhealthy?

2. How would you define a healthy spirituality?

3. What are your current core values?

4. Are there any areas of your life which do not align with your values?

5. Which spiritual practice are you finding life-giving just now?

6. What does a healthy spiritual community look like for you?

Wherever you are on your own journey, I hope this offering helps you travel further in love.

About the author

Andrea Gardiner grew up in Kent, England. She had a Christian upbringing in a Baptist church, and was educated at Ashford School for Girls, and Edinburgh Medical School. She graduated as a medical doctor in 2000, and now works as a General Practitioner. She also holds a BA(Hons) degree in Theology from the Open Theological College.

Andrea spent 13 rich years serving as a medical missionary in Ecuador, where she also ran a child sponsorship scheme and projects to build housing for the poor.

She currently resides in Scotland with her family.

You can find her at **www.returninghometoyourself.com**

Find her other titles on Amazon.co.uk including

Guinea Pig for Breakfast and Guinea Pig for Brunch – memoirs of working in Ecuador

Tamarita Rachel series of short stories set in the culture of Ecuador

Deepen – a mother – daughter Journal

Coming soon…. *Free Fall – a journal for an autumn season in life.*

Printed in Dunstable, United Kingdom